Haynes
Laptop
Manual

© Haynes Publishing 2007

All rights reserved. No part of this publication may be reproduced or
stored in a retrieval system or transmitted, in any form or by any means,
electronic, mechanical, photocopying, recording or otherwise, without
prior permission in writing from the publisher.

Published by: Haynes Publishing
Sparkford, Yeovil, Somerset BA22 7JJ
Tel: 01963 442030 Fax: 01963 440001
Int. tel: +44 1963 442030 Fax: +44 1963 440001
E-mail: sales@haynes.co.uk
Website: www.haynes.co.uk

British Library Cataloguing in Publication Data:
A catalogue record for this book is available from the British Library

ISBN 978 1 84425 439 2

Printed in Britain by J. H. Haynes & Co. Ltd., Sparkford

Throughout this book, trademarked names are used. Rather than put a
trademark symbol after every occurrence of a trademarked name, we use
the names in an editorial fashion only, and to the benefit of the trademark
owner, with no intention of infringement of the trademark. Where such
designations appear in this book, they have been printed with initial caps.

Whilst we at J. H. Haynes & Co. Ltd. strive to ensure the accuracy and
completeness of the information in this manual, it is provided entirely at the
risk of the user. Neither the company nor the author can accept liability for
any errors, omissions or damage resulting therefrom. In particular, users
should be aware that component and accessory manufacturers, and
software providers, can change specifications without notice, thus
appropriate professional advice should always be sought.

Haynes
Laptop
Manual

The step-by-step guide to upgrading,
repairing and maintaining a laptop

Haynes Publishing

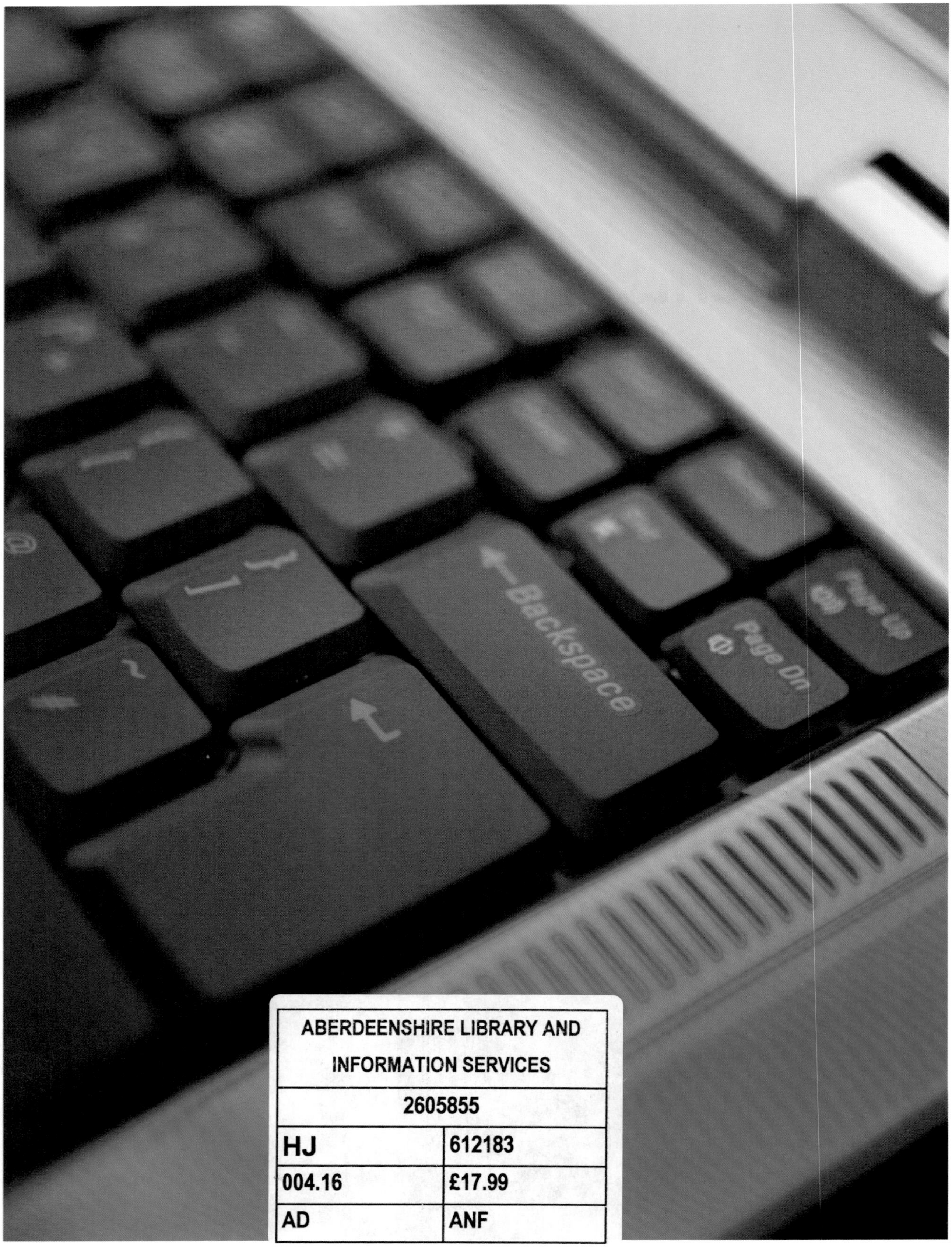
Backspace
Page Dn
Page Up

Contents

Introduction

Welcome to the first edition of the Laptop Manual. In this book, we cover everything you need to know about portable PCs: buying them, using them and improving them and what to do if your precious purchase packs up. If you're considering a portable computer but don't know what to buy or where to buy it, or if you're an experienced laptop user who needs to expand, upgrade or just eke every last drop of power from your laptop battery, this manual is for you.

Like all Haynes manuals, this book concentrates on what you actually need to know. We show you the things that matter (and make sure you don't spend money on things you don't need) and we never use jargon when we can explain things in plain English. Everything you'll read in these pages comes from years of real-

world experience, both good and bad – so, for example, when we discuss the right laptop for travelling, we've tried all kinds of machines on trains, buses and aeroplanes; when we talk about choosing the right laptop bag, our advice comes from years of lugging our laptops around endless airports and, in some cases, getting bruised shoulders because we bought a bad bag; and when we explore the wonders of wireless networking, we've used it in hotel lobbies, airport terminals and, on sunny days, our own back garden.

Everybody loves laptops

In 2007, laptop computers became the world's favourite machines, outselling their desktop siblings by a huge margin. That trend is set to continue: at the time of writing, desktop sales are growing by just 5% a year, but laptop sales are increasing by a massive 30% per year. That's not a big surprise: early laptops were incredibly expensive, incredibly heavy and offered battery life measured in minutes but today's machines are affordable, lightweight and can run for hours on a single charge.

So what's so great about laptops anyway?

They're portable

Today's sleek, light laptops are ideal for travellers. Business travellers can work on planes or in hotel rooms. If you're travelling for pleasure, you can use your machine to stay in touch by email or edit your holiday snaps while you're still on holiday. They're also ideal for business presentations, both face-to-face and to entire conferences.

They're small

Many people's laptops never leave the house. That's because they've been bought as desktop replacements. Even the smallest desktop PC takes up a fair bit of space and creates a Spaghetti Junction of cables, so space- or style-conscious computer users buy laptops instead. The same portability that makes laptops ideal for travel comes in handy at home too: you can surf the internet from your sofa, do a bit of clothes shopping from the kitchen table or order groceries from the garden. If we had moved our desktop PC around as much as we move our laptop, we'd have a hernia by now.

They're powerful

The days when laptops were a pale imitation of their desktop counterparts are long gone. Even the humblest laptop is perfectly capable of word processing, spreadsheets, email, internet browsing, organising your digital photos, managing your digital music… anything a desktop can do, a laptop can do too.

They're affordable

The price of laptops has plummeted in recent years. We're writing this on an ageing Apple PowerBook, which we bought four years ago for a terrifying £2,800. Last month, we bought an Acer machine that's just as fast as our ageing Apple and it cost £381. Of course, laptops can still be very expensive, but you don't need to spend thousands to get a good one.

They're connected

Almost every laptop has a network port that you can use to hook up to a hotel room's internet connections and lots of them also have wireless networking features (if your laptop doesn't, you can add an adapter for a few pounds). Wireless networks are proliferating, so for example you'll find them in coffee shops, motorway service stations, airports, hotels and even some bars.

Let's take a real world example. We're writing this chapter in an American hotel room, because we're in the US for a short business trip. Besides working on our documents, we've used our laptop to do some online banking, catch up with friends and colleagues by way of email, edit our digital photos and upload them to the internet, keep track of our various meetings and so on. On the flight over we used the laptop as a DVD player because the in-flight films were awful and since we've arrived we've used it as a digital jukebox that plays our favourite tunes.

We've also used it for some bargain hunting: at the moment the pound is worth around two dollars, so everything in the US is much, much cheaper than it is in Britain. We decided to get a new digital camera so we checked online to see which shops had bargains, turned to Google Maps to find out where they are and how to get there from our hotel, ordered online and reserved our camera for in-store pickup. The result? We've picked up a £400 digital camera for just £170 and we didn't have to wander from shop to shop to find it.

To put it another way: we could have done all of those things on our bargain basement, £381 Acer laptop – and that one bit of shopping saved us £230. Two bits of bargain hunting like that and your laptop has paid for itself!

Now we know why laptops are great, it's time to find out more about them. Over the page we'll discover the different shapes, sizes and systems available and how to decide which one is right for you.

PART **1** # How to pick the right laptop

Laptops: little and large

So you want to buy a laptop? Would that be a desktop replacement, a sub-notebook, an ultra-portable, a UMPC or a Tablet? Don't let the jargon confuse you – while there are all kinds of laptops available, the important thing is finding the one that's right for you. In this section, we discover the main kinds of machines you'll encounter and the pros and cons of each.

Let's get something out of the way first, though: from time to time you'll see laptops described as notebook computers. The terms 'laptop' and 'notebook' are interchangeable and they both mean the same thing: a portable computer. However, some other terms have specific meanings, so for example a UMPC is a specific kind of laptop and so is a Tablet PC. Let's find out more.

Desktop replacements

As the name suggests, a desktop replacement is designed to replace a desktop computer. Such machines tend to be among the biggest, most powerful laptops you can buy and naturally that means they can also be rather expensive. However, you do get a lot for your money. Desktop replacements typically have very big, very good quality displays, lots of expansion ports for plugging things in and very fast processors; the downside is that those big screens and fast processors need a lot of power, so battery life can be shorter than with other laptops. They also tend to be heavy, which is something you should think about if you're planning to take your laptop with you when you travel.

Gaming laptops

Gaming laptops are desktop replacements too, but they're designed for the demands of the latest PC games. That means

Gaming laptops such as Alienware's Aurora are designed to offer the maximum possible performance for today's ultra-demanding games. As you can imagine, they aren't cheap.

TECHIE CORNER

AMD or Intel?

Laptop processors are made by two companies: Intel and AMD. You don't need to worry about compatibility – Windows won't throw up its hands in horror at an AMD chip or anything like that – but it's important to know the differences between the two firms' product names unless you're buying a Mac, in which case your choice is Intel, Intel or Intel.

There are two kinds of processor to look out for: single core and dual core. The AMD Turion 64 X2 chip is a dual-core processor, which means that its processor essentially has two brains. It's the equivalent of Intel's Core 2 Duo chip, which is also a two-brainer. A plain old Turion 64 without the "X2" label, on the other hand, is a single core processor, as is Intel's Core Solo.

So what does this all mean? Dual core processors are faster than single core ones running at the same speed, so you'll tend to find that cheaper laptops have Turion 64s or Core 2 Solos while their more expensive siblings pack Core 2 Duos or Turion 64 X2s.

A direct speed comparison between AMD and Intel isn't possible on paper, because the different firms' chips work in different ways. However, websites such as Tom's Hardware (**www.tomshardware.co.uk**) run head-to-head tests between similarly specified AMD and Intel-powered laptops.

Tablet PCs are enormously clever. At first glance they're laptops, but the screen twists and they become touch-screen tablets for mobile working.

they tend to be the fastest laptops money can buy – and you'll need a lot of money to buy one. Once again, big screens and fast processors mean unimpressive battery life and portability isn't usually a major consideration so they can be very, very heavy.

Sub-notebooks and ultra-portables

Designed specifically for travellers, sub-notebooks and ultra-portables are designed with portability as the number one priority. That means they have excellent battery life and are very lightweight, but it also means smaller screens and slower processors. They're fantastic in cramped aeroplane seats or busy train carriages, but they're not as fast or as versatile as their bigger brothers.

UMPCs

UMPC stands for ultra-mobile PC and it's not to be confused with run-of-the-mill ultra-portables. UMPCs are based on designs from Microsoft and they're tiny but fully-featured Windows machines. Battery life is usually excellent but the screens and keyboards are positively titchy and it would be a very bad idea to use a UMPC as a desktop replacement. They can be very expensive too.

Tablet PCs

Another Microsoft design, the Tablet PC is designed for business users and students. Although it looks like a laptop, it has a clever trick up its sleeve. The screen is touch-sensitive and rotates, so besides using it as a laptop, you can use it like a clipboard. The computer automatically turns your handwriting into typed text and you can navigate by jabbing the screen with the stylus (or if you lose the stylus, which you will, with a biro). Just remember to keep the lid on or you'll cover your expensive screen with scratches and ink. They're fantastically clever but they're much heavier and much more expensive than normal laptops.

Laptops that aren't really laptops

As mobile phones get cleverer, the lines between phones and laptops are beginning to blur. For example, HTC, which makes phones such as the O2 XDA range, has a number of mobile phones with slide-out or flip-up keyboards. Such machines are fine for email or editing the odd document but they're phones first and computers second and those tiny keyboards are horrible to type on for more than a few minutes.

Computer compromises

As you can see, there are several compromises involved with laptops – machines that are designed for portability aren't as powerful as those designed to sit on your desk, while the most portable machines aren't as expandable as their bigger counterparts. These are the main compromises you'll need to think about.

Big screens

Great for everyday computing, but they need more power than smaller ones so battery life suffers. Big-screen laptops are heavier than small-screen ones and they're usually more expensive too.

Expansion slots

The smaller the laptop, the less likely you'll find connectors for every conceivable device. As a rule of thumb, the bigger the machine, the more USB ports and other connectors you'll get. Some laptops can run a second monitor simultaneously – great in the office, where you can have a twin-screen setup with the laptop running its own display as well as a desktop display and great for presentations where you can have your notes on your own screen but your presentation on a connected monitor or projector – but cheaper, smaller laptops don't always have that feature.

Power

The faster the laptop, the more power it needs and the shorter the battery life. As you'd expect, faster machines are more expensive than more modest ones. Gaming laptops are particularly expensive and, unless you're the sort of person who takes a laptop to a computer game convention for some multi-player action, they're almost certainly a bad buy.

Portability

Little screens and tiny keyboards are brilliant if you're stuck in a cramped seat on a Ryanair plane, but they're not much fun if you're going to use them for protracted periods.

Remember too that unlike desktop PCs, laptops have limited room for upgrades – so it's important to consider not just what you want your machine to do now, but what you want it to do next year. We'll look at upgrades and expansion later in this manual and we'd strongly advise against buying any machine until you've read that bit!

Before we continue, it's worth mentioning something that will make laptop firms cry: if you're buying a laptop for travelling, it's not always the best idea to buy a really expensive, do-everything machine – not least because there's always the risk of it being damaged or stolen on your travels. Before you decide that a £2,500 laptop is ideal for the odd business trip, ask yourself whether a cheapie would do the same job just as well.

PART 1

The big issue: Mac versus PC

Besides the various laptop designs, you've also got a choice of PC laptops – which run Microsoft Windows – or Apple Mac laptops, which don't (actually, it's a bit more complicated than that, as we'll explain in a moment). In some cases the choice will be made already, so for example if you fancy a Tablet PC then you need to buy a Windows machine, because Apple doesn't make tablet PCs. But if you don't want a Tablet PC, how do you choose between the two?

The choice used to be easy: Apple laptops were very sexy but really expensive and PC ones looked terrible but cost much less. However, the lines have blurred a lot and Apple now makes very affordable machines, while PC firms have raised their game and make some stunning – and in some cases, stunningly expensive – portable PCs.

There are two key differences between a Mac and a PC. The first is that Apple makes Macs and nobody else does, whereas PCs are made by everybody – Dell, Sony, HP and so on – so there's a much wider range of machines and a much wider range of prices to choose from if you go down the PC road. For example, if you want a Mac laptop you have a choice of two: the MacBook and the MacBook Pro. If you want a PC laptop there's Sony's Vaio range, Dell's Inspirons, Acer's Aspire and TravelMate ranges, Lenovo's Thinkpads...you get the idea, we're sure.

The other issue you need to consider is the operating system. PCs run Windows but Macs run a different system called Mac OS X.

Mac OS X

Windows Vista

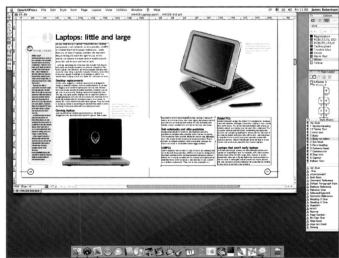

OS X explained

The operating system acts as a bridge between your hardware and your software, so for example when you hit the print button in Microsoft Word, the operating system says to the hardware: 'Here's a document. Can you send it to the printer, please?' It takes care of the basic but essential stuff from communicating with peripherals – your screen, your sound card, and so on – to file management, CD burning, networking, power management, and so on. However, while every operating system does essentially the same job, different systems take slightly different approaches and programs written for one operating system won't run on a different operating system.

So what does that mean for you? If you go for a Windows PC you won't be able to run any software written for Mac OS X and, until very recently, if you bought a Mac, you wouldn't be able to run Windows software. However, that's changed and you can use Windows on a Mac – for a price.

To run Windows programs on a Mac, you need to do one of two things. The first option is to use Apple's Boot Camp feature, which enables you to install a full copy of Windows on your Mac and then choose between Mac OS X or Windows on startup. The second option is to buy a program called Parallels Desktop and run Windows from inside Mac OS X. Whichever option you go for, though, you need to buy a full copy of Windows and any Windows programs you want to run. That could be quite expensive.

As most of the big-name programs – including Microsoft Office – are available for both Windows and OS X, we think the choice between a Windows PC and a Mac is largely down to personal preference. We use and like both. However, if you're on a really tight budget, you'll find that PC laptops can be much cheaper than Apple ones. Although Apple hardware is much cheaper than it used to be, a basic Mac laptop starts at around £680, while a basic PC laptop can be half that. You'll find similar price differences in the second-hand and refurbished markets too.

Enough theory – let's have a look at some laptops.

Mac users can run Windows on their machines using the free Boot Camp program, which ships with OS X – but you'll need to buy a copy of Windows too.

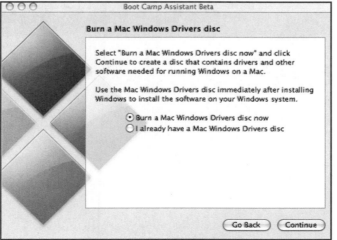

PART 1 A typical PC laptop

As we've already discovered, laptops come in all shapes and sizes. However, you tend to find similar features on every manufacturer's machines, so over the next few pages we'll show you the key features of a Windows laptop and an Apple one.

This is a fairly typical PC laptop – in this case, an Acer Aspire. The keyboard and screen dominate the machine and you'll see that there's also a trackpad in front of the keyboard that does the job a mouse would normally do. Some laptops have a little joystick instead of a trackpad. So which is best? We think they're both horrible things and we'd recommend an external mouse wherever possible.

Most PC laptops have a trackpad with two buttons, but our Acer has an extra rectangle between the trackpad buttons. These are navigation keys that enable you to quickly move left, right, up and down.

Above and to the left of the keyboard you'll also see a little row of keys. The first of these keys is Acer's e-key, which provides quick access to common system settings and to the right of that is a button that launches your email program. It contains an LED that lights up when you have new messages. Then there's a button to launch your web browser and finally there's the P button. This can be programmed to launch anything you like and the software to do this comes installed on the laptop when you buy it.

Like most laptops, the Acer uses the keyboard to control its hardware by way of the Function (Fn) key – so for example pressing Fn and then the arrow keys adjusts the display brightness.

Turn the laptop upside down and you'll see that there's a large battery running all the way across the back of the machine. You'll also see the official Windows certificate, which proves that there's a legitimate copy of Windows on the computer. And that's about it, so let's turn the laptop the right way up again.

This is the laptop shown from the front, with the lid closed. In the centre of the lid is a latch; to open the laptop, you need to slide the latch and lift the lid.

Let's take a closer look at that front panel. At the front left of the laptop are two LED lights. The LED on the left glows when the laptop is on and the LED on the right glows orange when your power cable is connected and the battery is recharging. Once your battery is fully charged, this LED glows green; if you disconnect the power cable, it goes dark.

Acer laptops have two kinds of wireless support: Wi-Fi wireless networking and Bluetooth for connecting to mobile phones and other small devices. Rather sensibly, Acer has decided to give you the ability to switch these features on and off without having to dig about in various Windows system options.

It's worth noting that the presence of a switch doesn't necessarily mean that the related hardware is installed, so for example this laptop has a switch for turning Bluetooth on and off but it doesn't contain any Bluetooth hardware – so the switch is utterly useless. That's because, to keep their costs down, many laptop manufacturers use the same laptop cases for an entire product range. That's certainly the case with this Acer laptop, which has the same casing as more expensive Bluetooth-enabled models but doesn't have the same features.

Besides its built-in speakers, the Aspire has an input for a microphone, an output for headphones and a digital output for connecting your laptop to your stereo.

There are two grilles on the front of the Acer and behind each one is a little speaker. Most laptop speakers are fine for the odd bit of audio and Acer's ones are by no means bad, but they're not really up to the job of listening to loud music or getting the best from film soundtracks – which is why there are headphone and line-out connectors too.

Now let's look at the right side.

This side of the case is dominated by a CD/DVD player and burner, which pops out when you press the switch on the drive door. Beside that is the modem connector, a standard telephone line connector that you can use if you're faxing from your laptop or if you want to connect to the internet using a normal phone line. Last but not least, at the very far right of the panel there's the socket for the power cable.

Time to spin the laptop round again, this time so we can have a look at the back panel.

On the very left of the back panel is a slot for a laptop lock, which you can use to tether your machine to something solid and to the right of that are twin USB ports for connecting keyboards, mice, digital cameras and other gadgets. At the far right of the

back panel, you'll see an Ethernet port, which you can use to connect an Ethernet cable to join a wired network or connect your laptop to a wired internet connection.

You'll see that, immediately before the Ethernet port, there's a blanking plate. Once again that's because the firm uses the same case for an entire product range, so more expensive laptops might have another connector – most likely a DVI video adapter – where our laptop has a bit of black plastic.

Finally we have the left side panel. There are several useful things here: the first port is the video connector, a standard VGA socket that enables you to connect your laptop to an external display or a projector. To the right of that there's a big grille and that's where hot air wafts out of your laptop and into the open air. It's a very bad idea to cover that up.

After the air vent there's an S-Video connector that you can use to connect the laptop to a television or a projector and next to that there's the third and final USB port. Finally you'll see two empty slots: the little one is a card reader for memory cards (such as digital camera cards) and the bigger one is a PC card slot. You can't expand a laptop by installing a PCI card, as you can in a desktop PC, because laptops simply don't have room. However, you can get the same effect by installing PC Card peripherals instead. Examples of such cards include wireless network adapters for PCs that don't have Wi-Fi equipment built-in or mobile data cards for super-fast internet access by way of the mobile phone network.

Multi-card readers are becoming a familiar sight in Windows laptops and they're wonderful things if, like us, you have a number of different devices that use memory cards but which don't use the same kinds of card. For example, our mobile phone uses SD memory cards, our big digital camera takes CompactFlash cards and our pocket camera takes something else entirely. With a multi-card reader you don't need to bother connecting your devices with cables to copy files to or from them: just take out the memory card, pop it into your PC and you're ready to go. Card readers are particularly good for photography, as they enable you to transfer your photos to your PC and then wipe the card so it's ready for even more shooting. As we discover later, you can also use them for Windows Vista's ReadyBoost feature, which can help smooth the performance of a laptop that's running out of memory.

Now we know our way around a Windows laptop, let's have a look and see if there are any key differences between PC laptops and Apple ones.

PART **1** # A typical Apple laptop

This is an Apple MacBook Pro, Apple's top-end laptop for demanding users and people with lots of cash. As we'll see, there are a few differences between Windows and Mac laptops, but they have lots in common too.

The most obvious difference you'll notice isn't Mac-specific: it's because of budget. While the MacBook Pro's brushed aluminium case looks much nicer than our Acer's horrible plastic, that's because the Mac costs nearly four times more than the Acer. If you spend the same on a Windows laptop you can expect a similarly attractive case, so for example Sony makes some very nice machines out of carbon fibre and other manufacturers use metal or glossy, high-impact plastic.

Once again the laptop is dominated by the keyboard and screen and once again there's a touch-sensitive trackpad at the front of the laptop that does the job a mouse would normally do. Apple makes two versions of its displays: the matte version shown here, which is non-reflective and a glossier version that delivers more vivid colours but which can suffer from glare if the room you're in is too bright. The choice comes down to personal preference, although we think for business use the matte display is best while the glossy screen is best suited to home use. There's no difference in price between a MacBook Pro with a matte or a glossy display.

As with the Acer, some keys control the hardware. For example, pressing F1 dims the screen and F2 brightens it.

There's one big difference between the trackpad on a Windows machine and one on an Apple laptop: Macs only have a single button. The same applies to Apple mice, too: where Windows loves you to right-click, Apple expects you to manage with just one mouse or trackpad button. As with our PC laptop we'd recommend using an external mouse anyway and if you buy a mouse with two or more buttons you can right-click to your heart's content. We use a 7-button Logitech mouse with our Mac and it works perfectly.

The little square in the top of the lid is an integrated iSight camera, which means you can use your Mac for video chat and other video applications without buying any additional hardware. It's no substitute for a proper grown-up digital camera, but it's fine for videoconferencing – although if your laptop is sitting on the desk with the camera pointing up towards you, don't be surprised if you look a bit chinny!

Flip the MacBook Pro upside down and you'll see that, just like a Windows laptop, there isn't really much to see other than the battery compartment. Here, it's at the bottom right.

Compared to the Acer, the Apple's front panel is extremely sparse. The button in the middle is a magnetic latch; if you press it, the lid pops up. The button also includes a little white LED that pulses when your Mac is in sleep mode. To the left of that is a little circle: that's the receiver for the Apple Remote Control, which you can use to control your Mac's music and video software.

The large grey slot at the right is a SuperDrive. Instead of the pop-out CD/DVD drives you'll find on most PC laptops, Apple's SuperDrive is a bog-standard CD/DVD player and burner that Apple's hidden inside the case. That means instead of a pop-out door, all you see is the slot to put your disc into. There's no eject button; you do that by pressing a key on the keyboard when your Mac's running.

Now let's look at the right of the MacBook Pro.

As you can see, there's a lot going on here. Let's take a closer look.

The little hole at the left is a slot for a laptop lock and immediately to the right of that is a USB port. There's only one USB port on this side of the machine. Next up are two FireWire ports, a USB-style connection that's used for high-speed devices such as video cameras, fast external hard disks and so on. There are two different standards – FireWire 400 and FireWire 800 – and the MacBook Pro has one connector for each.

After the FireWire ports, there's an Ethernet networking connector but no modem socket: Apple reckons that these days, everyone's using broadband or Wi-Fi wireless networking (which Apple calls AirPort). They're probably right. The strange-looking rectangle to the right of the Ethernet port is a DVI video connector. DVI is the successor to the old VGA video standard and it's designed to deliver the best possible quality to today's digital displays – but if your monitor, projector or television expects you to use a VGA cable then there's a DVI to VGA converter in the Mac's box.

This bit isn't important, but we think it's interesting: Apple's legendary attention to detail means that even its expansion ports have been arranged in the most attractive way possible.

The back of the MacBook Pro is completely blank – it's just the hinge for the display – so let's turn our attention to the left side panel. As you can see, it's fairly sparse. Let's look closer.

The socket at the very left of this panel only appears on Mac laptops and Apple calls it the Mag-safe power connector. It's all too easy to trip over the power cable when your laptop's charging and if you're unlucky it could send you and the laptop crashing to the floor – something that could prove painful financially as well as physically. Apple reckons it has solved the problem with its Mag-safe connectors, which automatically disconnect if they're jerked. As the name suggests, Mag-safe connections use magnetism to keep them in place.

Immediately to the right of the Mag-safe socket are another two USB ports and to the right of those are the two audio connectors: a line-in socket for a microphone and a line-out socket that doubles as a headphone socket.

Aha, you're thinking. That's a PC Card slot. You're nearly right – it's the PC Card slot's newer, smarter replacement called ExpressCard. As with PC Cards you can easily expand your machine by inserting a card, such as a modem card that uses the mobile phone network to get you online, but the newer ExpressCard standard offers better performance than the ageing PC Card standard.

Now we know what to expect from a laptop and what differences you'll find between Windows and Mac ones, it's time to cut to the chase. How much should you expect to pay for your laptop and what will you get for your money? Let's find out.

PART **1**

The price is right

Most manufacturers tend to put their laptops at particular price points, so there are broad similarities between different firms' products at the same prices. Here's what you can expect from a new laptop in the most popular price points.

Under £500

You should expect a decent all-rounder for this price – in the PC world at least (Mac laptops aren't available in this price bracket) – but don't expect the very fastest processors, very long battery life (you'll be lucky to get a battery that runs for more than an hour without needing to be recharged), a giant screen or a particularly stylish design. Inevitably corners will be cut to keep prices down, so hard disk capacities will be smaller and there will be less installed memory than in more expensive machines.

You'll typically find that the graphics card in the cheapest laptops uses shared memory, which means it's less powerful than a stand-alone graphics chip and it also means that the graphics card uses some of your system RAM. That can be a big issue if you're planning to run Windows Vista on a machine with 512MB of RAM: 512MB is the bare minimum for Vista and shared graphics memory means you'll fall below that minimum. It doesn't make a big difference for web browsing or word processing, but it's fatal for games or demanding tasks such as photo or video editing.

In many cases you'll also find that the operating system is the Home Basic edition of Windows Vista, which isn't as good as the slightly more expensive Home Premium edition.

Up to £1,000

This is the sweet spot for laptops: here you'll find decent processors, decent battery life, a reasonable amount of installed memory and in some cases, 17 inch widescreen displays. Instead of Home Basic, you get Windows Vista Home Premium, the graphics card is a stand-alone model instead of one that uses system RAM and hard disk capacities are decent. You'll also find many sub-notebooks and Tablet PCs in this price range, along with Apple's entry-level MacBook laptop.

Over £1,000

Once you crack the £1,000 mark you're entering the world of cutting-edge technology. Processors and hard disks are faster, graphics cards are more powerful, the displays are bigger and brighter and the hard disks offer more storage and faster speeds. You'll find gaming laptops in this price bracket, as well as the ultra-light sub-notebooks and multimedia PCs and, in Apple territory, the MacBook is replaced by the more powerful MacBook Pro.

Over £1,500

Only the very brave spend more than £1,500 on a new laptop, because such machines offer the very latest everything – which means that six months after you buy it, the same technology will have filtered down to laptops costing half the price. However, if you want the best of everything right now then you'll find it in this price range. Laptops in this price bracket have the very fastest processors, lots of memory, the most powerful graphics cards and the biggest, fastest hard disks and they usually have the most powerful batteries too.

Example laptops

Let's have a look at some real examples. As ever, details are correct at the time of going to print but this is a fast-moving market, so the cutting-edge computer of today will look positively prehistoric in six months' time.

Dell Inspiron 1501, £429

What you get: AMD Turion 64 X2 processor, 1GB RAM, 15.4 inch widescreen display, 80GB hard disk, integrated graphics card, DVD writer and Microsoft Works software.

Need to know: This machine offers a very generous specification and AMD's Turion processors offer good performance, but corners have been cut to keep the price down. The biggest such corner is the battery. This battery is one of the worst Dell offers with a very short life (it is rated at 29 watt hours, compared to 54 watt hours for other batteries and around 80 watt hours for Dell's best batteries), so it's not ideal for travelling. The graphics card uses shared memory but that's not a huge problem, as there's a decent 1GB of RAM.

Apple MacBook 13-inch, £879

What you get: Intel Core 2 Duo 2GHz processor, 1GB RAM, 13 inch glossy display, 80GB hard disk, integrated graphics card and DVD writer.

Need to know: Another excellent all-rounder, Apple's MacBook is a good travel companion although integrated graphics means it's not the most powerful machine. The processor's quick, though, and you also get Apple's excellent iLife software for photo editing, making DVDs and managing your music collection.

Sony VAIO FE41Z, £1,165

What you get: Intel Core 2 Duo 2GHz processor, 2GB RAM, 15.4 inch X-Black widescreen display, 200GB hard disk, stand-alone Radeon graphics card and DVD writer.

Need to know: We're moving into performance laptop territory now and this Sony's really rather quick thanks to its fast processor, 2GB of memory and dedicated graphics chip. The only thing that lets it down is the hard disk which, while big, runs at a fairly slow 4,200RPM. Typical performance laptop drives run at 5,400rpm or higher. However, that's a minor blemish on an otherwise superb machine.

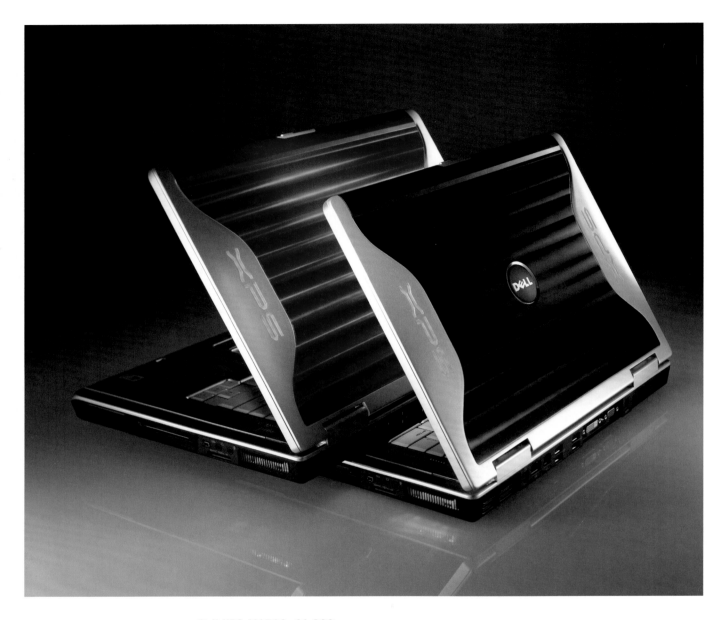

Dell XPS M1710, £1,399

What you get: Intel Core 2 Duo 2.16GHz processor, 1GB RAM, 17 inch ultrasharp widescreen display, 160GB hard disk, standalone GeForce graphics card with 512MB RAM and DVD writer.

Need to know: Fancy a gaming laptop? Look no further. While most performance laptops have 256MB graphics cards this Dell has double that amount, making it ideal for gaming. You get Dell's best battery, a reasonable amount of RAM and a decent hard disk, but if you really want to push the boat out you can specify a faster processor, 4GB of RAM and a faster hard disk – although that takes the final price to nearly £3,000.

Sony VAIO VGN-TX3XP/B, £1,292

What you get: Intel Core Solo 1.03GHz processor, 512MB RAM, 11.1 inch X-black widescreen display, 80GB hard disk, integrated graphics card, DVD writer and memory card reader.

Need to know: It's not cheap and it's hardly the fastest laptop in the world, so why is this VAIO so expensive? It's made largely of carbon fibre, which means a titchy weight of just 1.3kg. Factor in up to 7 hours of battery life and a tiny but beautiful 11.1-inch display and you've got a superb machine for long-distance travelling.

Apple MacBook Pro 17 inch, £1,899

What you get: Intel Core 2 Duo 2.33GHz processor, 2GB RAM, 17 inch widescreen display, 160GB hard disk, stand-alone Radeon graphics card and DVD writer.

Need to know: Apple's most expensive laptop is faster than any desktop iMac, with the fastest Core 2 Duo chip and dedicated graphics card delivering blistering performance. If you're feeling really adventurous you can specify extra memory and a bigger hard disk, taking the price to a truly terrifying £2,348.99.

PART ① Case studies: who needs what

So what kind of laptop should you be looking for? As you'd expect, that depends on what kind of user you are. Let's look at five very different kinds of computer user to see what kind of kit best suits their needs.

The transatlantic traveller

We recommend: an ultra-portable laptop with very low weight and a small screen

The transatlantic traveller spends more time on jumbo jets than in the office and portability is key. While business class seats have plenty of room, a laptop with a giant 17 inch screen is too big to use comfortably in an aircraft seat. A Tablet PC or better still, an ultra-light, ultra-small laptop would be ideal for the traveller who needs to work or watch DVDs on the move, not least because he or she will spend almost as long carrying the laptop around as using it.

For business travellers, battery life isn't a big issue. That's because of two things: no laptop battery can last all the way from London to Los Angeles and most major airlines have power sockets in business class seats. That means business travellers can buy a relatively cheap power adapter and keep their laptop on mains power throughout the flight.

The road warrior

We recommend: integrated wireless networking and extra-long battery life

The road warrior's office canteen is the motorway service station and that often means catching up on email while grabbing a quick sandwich. Portability and performance aren't big issues here but battery life is: using wireless networks in public hotspots is a notorious battery drainer and if you're giving presentations to potential clients you can't be sure that you'll be near a power socket when you deliver your PowerPoint presentation. A laptop with integrated wireless networking and a good clear screen is a must, although we'd steer clear of machines with glossy displays. Road warriors can't always be sure of working or presenting in a glare-free environment and matte displays cope better in poor lighting conditions than glossy ones do.

The gamer

We recommend: the fastest processor, lots of RAM and a huge screen

For PC gamers, it's all about performance – the only reason they're lugging a laptop is because they're taking it to multiplayer gaming events where they can battle like-minded people. That means battery life isn't an issue – the laptop will be plugged in when the games are being played – and weight doesn't matter

either, because the laptop won't do much travelling. The gamer will be looking for the fastest possible processor and hard disk, a big screen with a powerful graphics card and stacks of RAM. Really keen gamers will head directly for specialist manufacturers, such as Alienware, which make performance laptops designed specifically for the PC gaming community.

The family

We recommend: a big screen, plenty of USB ports and a huge hard disk

Family laptops spend most of their time running on mains power and sitting on a desk, so weight and battery life aren't an issue – but a nice big screen, plenty of USB ports and a big hard disk are essential. The USB ports will come in handy for connecting digital cameras, camcorders, iPods, webcams, printers, satellite navigation systems and all the other gadgets your family members will want to use and a small hard disk will quickly fill to bursting point with even a modest library of digital photos and home videos.

Both Windows and OS X enable you to create separate accounts for each family member, so for example you might have one username and password for you, one for your partner and one for each of the children. That's great because it means you can limit what each person can and can't do with the computer, such as limiting when the kids can use the internet, but it does mean you'll use considerably more hard disk space than a single-user machine. Even with large hard disks, keen camcorder users should seriously consider investing in an external hard drive, because video files are massive.

The student

We recommend: a mid-range, reasonably portable laptop with integrated wireless networking

Student laptops lead a double life. By day they're used in lectures, but by night they're used for internet browsing, music and video. You don't need an ultra-fast processor for any of those things, but portability and decent battery life are important, as is plenty of hard disk space for storing music, movies and digital photos. Built-in wireless networking will come in handy too, because many educational establishments and their nearby halls of residences, bars, libraries and coffee shops offer wireless internet access.

PART **1**

How to buy your kit

You know what you need, but where should you buy it? While it's possible to nip down to your local computer shop and stock up on computers, printers and other essential equipment, it's not always the best – or the cheapest – way to do it.

Where to buy computers

You can buy computers in any high street, but the stock is usually limited – and in many cases, you can find the same machines on the internet for considerably less cash. Some firms such as PC giant Dell don't sell their machines through the shops at all; instead, they sell machines over the phone or by way of their website (**www.dell.com/uk**). Because they don't have expensive high street premises to maintain they can often sell computers for much less than you'd pay in the shops.

You can certainly save money by buying online, but shops have their benefits too. One of the main ones is that if you have a problem, you don't need to send your computer back to Ireland (or Amsterdam, or wherever the manufacturer is based) for repair; if you buy from an independent retailer, you might get better after-sales service or support than from a giant corporation. You'll occasionally find that retailers offer more generous deals than manufacturers do, especially with firms such as Apple who don't allow retailers to offer discounts on their computers: for example at the time of writing John Lewis sells a range of Apple laptops whose price and specification are identical to the machines on Apple's own website, but where Apple offers a standard one-year warranty John Lewis offers two years for the same price.

High street shops aren't ideal for everybody, though. John Lewis' warranty is a great deal, but like every other retailer, it's in the business of selling what's on its shelves. That means your choice is limited to the configurations that the shop sells, so in many cases if you don't see it you can't have it. If you like a particular laptop but want a different configuration such as more memory, a different graphics card or a better optical drive, you might not be able to get it – and the same applies to many online computer shops too. If they don't build the machines they sell, you might not be able to change the configuration of your chosen machine.

If you know what you want, manufacturers' sites can be a better bet. Firms who build their machines to order enable you to customise every single component, so you can get a machine that meets your needs perfectly. The alternative – buying a laptop off the shelf and then upgrading it later – is usually much more expensive.

Of course, the main reason to buy online is price. When you compare high street prices with internet prices using a price comparison service such as Kelkoo (**www.kelkoo.com**), you'll see that you pay a hefty premium for the personal touch.

If you're buying a standard configuration, you might find that some retailers offer better deals than the manufacturers – so for example this John Lewis deal gives you twice the warranty for the same price as Apple's website.

Beware of bundles

Many PCs are sold as bundles: buy this machine and get a free printer, or digital camera, or some other bit of equipment. However, some deals are better than others. Bundled printers or digital cameras tend to be fairly unsophisticated models, whereas 'double memory for free!' deals are often worth taking advantage of. Don't let bundles blind you to the machine itself, though: if the machine isn't right for you, the inclusion of a printer you don't want and some software you'll never use won't make the computer any better.

It's worth being cynical about special offers too. Computer firms and retailers are a bit like sofa shops: as soon as one unmissable, buy-now-or-regret-it-forever deal ends, a new one pops up in its place. Many sales and special offers are designed to make way for brand new products, so if you do take advantage of a great deal you might find that a newer, better machine goes on sale before your laptop has even been delivered. That's the nature of computing, unfortunately, but under the UK Consumer Protection (Distance Selling) Regulations you do have seven days to change your mind after your computer has been delivered. We'll look at your rights in more detail in a moment.

Where to buy printers, network cards and other equipment

When it comes to computer add-ons such as printers, wireless networking gear or other equipment, the best place to buy is usually online: a Netgear router from a shop is identical to one from an online retailer and the difference in price can be dramatic. Savings of 30% compared to high street prices aren't unusual and if you use a site such as **www.Kelkoo.com** to check prices you can find the best deals with hardly any effort. However, make sure you're comparing like with like: some sites charge what seem to be very cheap prices, but then expect you to pay hefty postage fees; others don't include VAT or sell OEM (Original Equipment Manufacturer) versions that don't include packaging or manuals. Whether you're using a price checking service or browsing from shop to shop, make sure you're comparing the price you'll actually pay rather than the headline price.

As with computers, when you buy add-ons or consumables online you should always follow the golden rules: don't buy from sites you don't trust 100% and always pay with your credit card.

PART 1 How to pay for your laptop

When you buy a computer there are usually several ways to pay for it. You can pay up-front, take a finance deal or, if you're a limited company, you can lease the equipment.

Paying up-front is cheapest, but always use a credit card: that way if the company goes out of business before your machine arrives, or before the warranty expires, then you can file a claim with your credit card company to get your money back or to get the warranty honoured. That's because when you pay with credit cards (but not with debit cards such as Maestro cards or credit card cheques), two contracts are formed. Your contract is with the credit card company, not the retailer, so if the retailer doesn't fulfil its side of the deal then the credit card company is liable.

If you do pay by credit card, resist the temptation to leave the balance on your card. If you borrow £1,000 on a card and only make the minimum payment each month, depending on the card's interest rate it could take between 14 and 28 years to pay for your PC.

If you're buying from a shop in person, don't pay with cash – and especially, don't use your credit card to withdraw cash because you think you might be able to negotiate a cash discount. While you may well get a discount – businesses pay a few per cent of each sale when they accept credit cards – cash doesn't provide you with the same protection as paying by card.

It's important to note that credit cards won't protect you from some kinds of fraud: if you hand over your card details to a criminal, you're unlikely to get your money back. That's why if you shop online it's essential to use sites you trust. If you have the slightest doubt about a site, go elsewhere.

Of course, sometimes you will have to pay cash – for example, when you're buying a machine second-hand from the small ads. Whatever you do, don't use your credit card to get the money from a cash machine. Unlike card purchases, cash advances don't have an interest-free period (so interest starts accumulating from day one, whereas most card purchases are interest-free for 40 or 60 days) – and the interest rates are horrific. It's not unusual to discover that a low-rate credit card levies a whopping 24.9% on cash advances. Because your card repayments go to the lowest interest rates first – so your payment goes to any 0% offer, then to balance transfers, then to purchases and only then to cash advances – if you don't pay your balance in full immediately, any cash advance could end up accruing interest not just for weeks, but for years.

With finance deals you can spread the cost of a computer over 12, 24 or 36 months. Inevitably there's a cost for this and it's important to check the small print carefully. Many finance deals charge very high interest rates and it's often cheaper to get a personal loan from the bank or to use a credit card with a long 0% introductory offer.

https://www.capitalone.co.uk – Summary Box		

Capital One
Print Page Close Window

Key features of your Capital One credit card

SUMMARY BOX
The information contained in this table summarises key product features and is not intended to replace any terms and conditions.

APR	Typical **9.9 % APR** variable		
	Introductory rate	Monthly rate	Annual rate
Purchases	0.00 % until your May 2008 statement	0.79 %	9.94 %*
Balance Transfers	0.00 % until your May 2008 statement	0.79 %	9.94 %*
Cash withdrawals	N/A	1.94 %	25.94 %*
Interest free period	Maximum of 56 days for purchases where the balance is paid in full every month. 0 days for balance transfers and cash.		
Interest charging information	**Purchases, Balance transfers and Cash withdrawals** Whenever an interest free period does not apply, interest is charged to your account from the date of the transaction and will continue until the statement balance is paid in full. Interest is calculated daily on the account balance. Full details can be found in your Credit Card Agreement.		
Allocation of payments	If you do not pay off your balance in full when you make a payment it will be used to pay off in the following order: any cash handling fees; any interest; other fees; Payment Protection Insurance; most balance transfers except those described next; then balance transfers made after any initial period, if at the time, your initial period was described as "for the life of balances transferred", and all purchases; then cash withdrawals.		
Minimum repayment	3% of the outstanding balance or £5, whichever is greater.		
Amount of	Minimum credit limit of £1000; maximum credit limit £16000		

Done www.capitalone.co.uk

Here's why you shouldn't use your credit card to withdraw cash for a laptop purchase: while this credit card's interest rate is 0% on card purchases, cash withdrawals are charged at 25.94% and there's no interest-free period.

PART **1**

Buying online? Know your rights

In June 2007, the Office of Fair Trading found that 59% of UK internet shoppers didn't know about their rights under the Distance Selling Regulations and other consumer protection law – which is hardly surprising when two-thirds of UK-based traders weren't sure about the regulations either. That's worrying, because in some cases online shops have imposed illegal conditions on their customers.

If you're based in the UK and buying from a UK website, your rights under the Sale of Goods Act are enhanced considerably by the Distance Selling Regulations. So what bits of the law do online shops tend to get wrong? Here are some of the more common things that online shops – wrongly – tell their customers.

You can't cancel your order once seven days have passed.
The Consumer Protection (Distance Selling) Regulations give you a seven-day cooling-off period. That period starts when your computer is delivered, not when you order it.

You can't cancel your order just because it hasn't been delivered yet.
Yes, you can. Unless agreed at the time of ordering, goods should be delivered within 30 days. If they aren't, you can cancel and get a full refund.

You can't return it. It isn't faulty.
During the seven-day cooling off period, you can cancel your order for any reason at all.

We'll collect it, but you have to pay for that.
Not if the goods are faulty, you don't. Firms can impose a reasonable fee for collecting returned goods, but only if that's clearly stated in their terms and conditions at the time of ordering. They cannot charge you if you're returning goods because they're faulty.

There's a restocking fee for returns if goods aren't faulty.
Such fees are illegal. The company can charge for collection if you cancel within the seven-day cooling-off period, but that's the only fee they can charge – and they need to mention that fee in their terms and conditions.

You can't return it. It's a custom-built machine.
In the eyes of the Office of Fair Trading, a computer built to order from a selection of standard components is not a personalised item.

As you can see, when you buy online you benefit from a huge amount of protection – but only when you buy from UK businesses so, for example, the Distance Selling Regulations don't cover you if you buy a laptop from an individual on eBay.
Did we say eBay?

Auction fever: buying laptops on eBay

Online auction sites such as eBay (**www.ebay.co.uk**) and QXL (**www.qxl.com**) can be a great source of bargains, but there are risks: when the hammer falls, you can't change your mind. Because you can't pop round to the seller's house and see a laptop before pledging your cash, it's essential that you know exactly what you're bidding for.

With online auctions you need to read the item descriptions carefully and if anything is unclear, ask lots of questions. Use the seller's feedback rating to get an idea of his or her trustworthiness; if the seller is new to the site and has no feedback from previous auctions it doesn't mean they're dodgy, but it does mean you should be very careful and ask lots of questions about the machine, its history, whether the seller has the original software discs and so on.

Make sure the machine is actually in the UK and is a UK-specification machine, too: imports are worth less money and if your computer is being shipped from the US there's an increased risk of damage in transit. You're also liable for VAT and other duty on any purchase from outside the EU; for a £1,000 laptop that could add several hundred pounds to the price tag. There have also been a number of cases of auction fraud involving sellers from Eastern Europe who ask for cash payments or bank credit transfers: another good reason to stick with UK sellers.

The risk of fraud is minimal – eBay claims that less than 0.01% of auction sales are fraudulent – but it's still a risk: while every eBay transaction that uses the PayPal payment system is covered by the PayPal Buyer Protection Programme, it will only pay compensation of up to £150 for normal purchases and £500 for goods sold by PayPal-approved sellers and you have to follow very strict rules to qualify (**http://pages.ebay.co.uk/help/tp/paypal-protection.html**). If you have the slightest doubt about the seller or the item they're selling then don't place a bid.

Beware of commercial traders pretending to be normal users: the average person doesn't have the capability to accept credit card payments, so if a supposedly private seller can take Mastercard or Visa (without using an intermediary such as PayPal or NoChex) then they're probably a commercial operation. There are plenty of traders on auction sites who are honest, but the ones who pretend to be private sellers are trying to evade the Distance Selling Regulations and the Sale of Goods Act.

We'd strongly recommend the use of an escrow service, too. With normal auctions the process is simple: you pay the seller and the seller ships the goods. However, with big ticket items such as laptops that's a fairly risky procedure and it's possible that the seller could take your cash and do a disappearing act. To prevent this, an escrow service will charge you a small fee to act as a middleman. You lodge your payment with the escrow service and the seller doesn't get the cash until the goods have been delivered. If you're planning to spend several hundred pounds on a computer and the seller isn't willing to use the escrow service – even if you pay the escrow fee – then it should once again set alarm bells ringing.

Finally, beware of auction fever. Many people end up paying over the odds because they think that if it's an auction sale, it must be a bargain; in some cases, laptops sell for more money than brand new models cost in online shops. Do your homework, research prices and identify the going rate for your chosen hardware, then set a budget and stick to it.

eBay can be a great place to pick up laptops for low prices, but you need to be very careful to make sure you don't fall for a scammer. There is a fraud compensation scheme but its maximum payout is less than the cost of a half-decent laptop.

---

eBaY .co.uk Sign in or register

Search | Advanced Search   **Buy** | Sell | My eBay | Community | Help

Site Map

Categories ▾ | Shops

Back to homepage

Listed in category: <u>Computing</u> > <u>Apple/ Macintosh</u> > <u>MacBook</u>
Also listed in: <u>Computing</u> > <u>Laptops</u>

Apple MacBook Pro 2.33GHz
Power & performance in a Stylish Package

Item number: 190132879454

Bidder or seller of this item? <u>Sign in</u> for your status

<u>Watch this item</u> in My eBay

Current bid: £770.00   **Place Bid >**

End time: **1 hour 52 mins** (24-Jul-07 15:01:16 BST)
Postage costs: **£20.00**
                 Parcelforce 48
                 Service to <u>United Kingdom</u>
                 (<u>more services</u>)
Post to: United Kingdom
Item location: Edinburgh, United Kingdom
History: <u>21 bids</u>
High bidder: <u>Bidder 12</u> ☆

You can also: Watch This Item

Get alerts via <u>Text message</u> or <u>IM</u>
<u>Email to a friend</u>

<u>View larger picture</u>

Meet the seller
Seller: <u>louis_tabasco</u> (2)
Feedback: **100% Positive**
Member: since 06-Jan-02 in United Kingdom
▪ <u>Read feedback comments</u>
▪ <u>Ask seller a question</u>
▪ <u>Add to Favourite Sellers</u>
▪ <u>View seller's other items</u>

Buy safely
1. **Check the seller's reputation**
   Score: 2 | 100% Positive
   <u>Read feedback comments</u>

2. **Check how you're protected**
   PayPal Choose PayPal for up to £150 buyer protection. <u>See terms & conditions</u>

Listing and payment details: <u>Show</u>

Description (<u>revised</u>)

Item Specifics - Apple Laptops			
Product Family:	**MacBook Pro**	Hard Drive Capacity:	**120 GB**
Processor Type:	--	Operating System:	**Mac OS 10.4, Tiger**
Processor Speed:	--	Screen Size:	**15 inches**
Memory (RAM):	**2,000 MB**	Condition:	**Used**

Item Specifics - PC Laptops			
Brand:	--	Condition:	**Used**
Processor Speed:	**2.3 GHz**	Processor Type:	--
Hard Drive Capacity:	**120 GB**	Memory (RAM):	**2 GB**
Screen Size:	**15 inches**	Primary Drive:	**DVD+/-RW**

PART **1**

Scouring the small ads

As with auctions, most small-ad sellers are perfectly reputable; however, when you consider that 67,000 laptops were stolen in the UK in 2004 alone, it's sensible to be suspicious. Not all stolen machines are sold in pubs or from the backs of lorries.

It's important to tread carefully with second-hand equipment because if you buy a machine privately and something goes wrong, you're not protected by consumer legislation. The Sale of Goods Act does apply to private sales, but only in a limited way: the goods must be safe and 'as described'; if not, you have the right to seek a refund. In practice, getting a refund from a private seller may require a trip to the courts.

So what should you look for? Beware of dodgy dealers. These are people in the PC sales business who pretend to be private advertisers. In many cases they do this to avoid paying tax, but in some cases they are doing it so you don't have any comeback should your purchase pack up. Tell-tale signs are adverts offering new, boxed machines – would you buy a brand new laptop and sell it without even taking it out of the packaging? – or adverts offering multiple machines; see if the same phone number appears on different ads and look for any mention of VAT. Private customers neither know nor care about VAT, but traders do. Remember that it's illegal for traders to pose as private sellers, so if they're willing to break that law you can't expect them to be honest about anything else.

It's essential that you see the computer for yourself before buying, either in the seller's home or workplace. Any other meeting place should set alarm bells ringing. When you get there check the screen for dead pixels, make sure that any connectors aren't bent and look for obvious signs of damage that might indicate the machine hasn't been well looked after. Check that any supplied peripherals (keyboards, mice, add-on cards) actually work and make sure the machine functions when it's unplugged from the mains – and that the battery charges when you plug it back in again.

Ask if the seller has the original receipt – many legitimate sellers will have – and make sure there are discs to match the supplied software. When you buy a computer, it's a very good idea to reformat the hard disc and reinstall the software and any necessary drivers; if you don't have the discs, you may have to buy Windows, Office and any other key programs. Be particularly wary of any seller offering big-name products such as Photoshop, Office or other goodies if they don't have the CDs: it's a good indication that the software is illegal. Most importantly, ask questions. If you feel the seller isn't telling the whole truth, take your money elsewhere.

PART **1**

Refurbs and clearances: the best of both worlds?

If you'd like the savings of second-hand equipment but don't fancy the risks, there are two other options: end-of-line stock and refurbished machines. You'll find end-of-line stock offered by firms such as Morgan Computers (**www.morgancomputers.com**), while Dell and Apple – not to mention independents such as Cancom UK (**www.cancomuk.com**) – sell refurbished machines.

If a computer is described as end-of-line stock, it means that that particular model has been discontinued – usually to make way for a newer, sleeker model. While some end-of-line stock is positively ancient, there are plenty of decent machines out there with very low price tags. If you don't need the very latest model, you can get a very powerful machine for surprisingly little money.

Refurbished machines – 'refurbs' for short – are slightly different. When Apple or Dell sells a machine, if it's returned with a minor fault they can't simply fix the problem and sell it as new. Instead, they shift the stock through firms such as Cancom UK (**www.cancomuk.com**) or through their own outlets – the Apple Refurb Store (**http://store.apple.com/Apple/ WebObjects/ukstore?promo=RefurbStore/**) and the Dell Outlet (**www1.euro.dell.com/content/default.aspx?c= uk&l=en&s=dfo**). Besides repaired machines, both outlets also sell returned stock from cancelled orders and occasionally, ex-lease equipment. The available discounts vary, but it's not unusual to see refurbs being sold with 45% off the list price.

When you're considering refurbished kit, it's important to know the potential downsides. Refurbs are rarely the most up-to-date models, so if you're expecting 45% off the very latest Apple MacBook Pro you'll probably be disappointed. In most cases you won't be able to finance your purchase, either: both Dell and Apple expect you to pay in full when you order.

Other things to consider are the machine's appearance – it's likely to have a few scratches or discoloration – and warranty support. If you buy from Cancom you get a three-month warranty (unless the product is marked as an Apple Refurb, in which case you get a 12-month warranty); buy direct from Dell or Apple and you get a standard one-year limited warranty. However, in most cases if your refurbished machine has a fault on arrival, you can't get it repaired or replaced; instead, the manufacturer will arrange for the machine to be returned and your money to be refunded.

Firms such as Apple sell refurbished machines at huge discounts, but don't expect the very latest models.

PART **2**

Using your laptop

As a laptop is simply a PC crammed into a portable case, when it comes to everyday activities it works in exactly the same way as a desktop model. However, laptops also need to worry about things desktop machines don't, such as battery life, instant access to applications and so on. As a result you'll find that your machine has a range of hardware and software features that can extend battery life, boost its performance or just get what you need quickly. In this section, we discover what they are and how they can make your laptop's life easier.

Desktop differences

There are two major differences between laptop and desktop PCs that we think you should consider. The first and most obvious difference is that your laptop crams keyboard, mouse (or trackpad) and display into a single box, which isn't always ideal for comfortable computing and which limits your expansion options. The second is that the more power you use, the less battery life you'll get. Let's discover what the issues are and what you can do about them.

Ergonomics

Computers really can damage your health. One key risk is repetitive strain injury (RSI), a catch-all term used to describe disorders such as carpal tunnel syndrome in the wrists, muscular pains in the neck and shoulders, and tendon damage in joints. In each case, over-use is a key factor and computer users – especially laptop users – are particularly at risk.

The RSI Association (**www.rsi.org.uk**) reports that every day, six people leave their jobs because RSI makes it impossible to keep working. It also affects the rest of your life: driving can be painful and even everyday tasks such as filling a kettle, doing the shopping or writing a letter can be excruciating. According to the RSI Association, one in 50 UK workers has reported an RSI-related condition and businesses lose 5.4 million working days due to RSI-related sick leave. In Australia, 60% of schoolchildren using laptops have reported discomfort and, in Holland, 40% of university students have an RSI condition.

To avoid RSI, posture is important. Your body should be at right angles – so for example when you type your back should be straight, your upper arms vertical and your forearms at 90 degrees – and your screen should be at eye level. That's easy enough with a desktop PC, but impossible with a laptop: you can raise the screen to eye level or place the computer on a desk for ergonomically correct typing, but you can't do both. There is a solution, though and that's to invest in a laptop stand to raise your screen to a better height. Simply plug in an external keyboard and mouse and your working area will be as comfortable – and as safe – as any desktop user's.

Turning your laptop into a desktop replacement

Laptop PCs are much easier to set up than desktop computers, not least because the screen is already connected to the computer. However, there are potential problems too – and the main one is that laptops have far fewer connectors than desktop PCs. As we'll discover in this walkthrough, that doesn't mean you can't connect all your devices: it just means you need to connect them in a slightly different way.

Laptops are much more flexible than desktop PCs, but there's a price to pay: fewer connections, such as USB ports.

1

It's a good idea to have a separate keyboard for your laptop if you'll be doing lots of typing. Some keyboards, such as this Dell one, come with wrist rests that are designed to make keyboarding more comfortable.

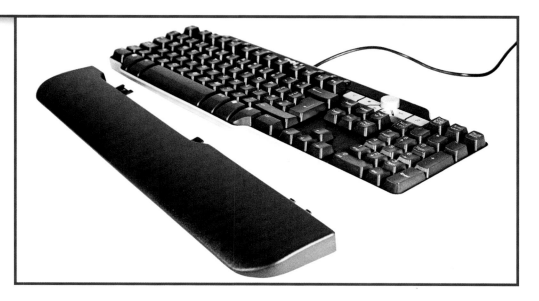

2

The wrist rest is designed to slot into the front of the keyboard, which has slots into which the wrist rest can clip. Fitting a wrist rest is easier if you turn the keyboard upside down to reveal the slots and then line up the clips with the slots.

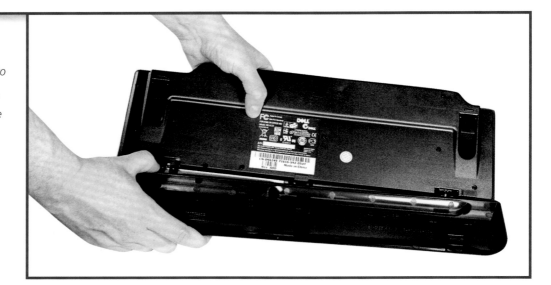

3

Once you've lined up the clips with the slots, press the wrist rest firmly (but not forcefully: the clips are fragile and if you push too hard you may break them) into place. Depending on the kind of keyboard you have, you might need to squeeze the clips slightly to do this. The wrist rest should now click securely into place.

4

As with a desktop PC's keyboard, the laptop keyboard needs to be plugged into a spare USB port. Locate the USB ports on your laptop (they'll be at the side or on the back of the case) and slot the keyboard connector into place.

The mouse needs to be connected to a USB port too, but rather than use up another of the laptop's precious USB ports we'll use one on the keyboard instead. With our keyboard, the USB ports are on the back, but with other models the ports are often on the left or right of the keyboard case.

The quickest way to get your laptop online at home or in the office is to connect it to your router, which is what we've done here. As with a desktop PC, simply plug one end of an Ethernet cable into the computer's Ethernet port and then plug the other end into your router.

The Centrino logo on a laptop means that all the necessary equipment for wireless networking is already inside the machine, so you won't need any additional hardware to take advantage of wireless networks at home or when you're on the move (provided that you have a wireless router that the laptop can connect to). We'll take a detailed look at wireless networking in Part 3.

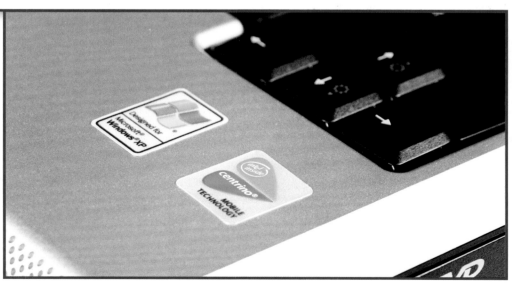

8

Finally you can connect the power. Although laptops are designed to run on batteries, those batteries don't last long – and if you connect external devices such as keyboards and mice, or if you use wireless networking, the battery life deteriorates further. Plugging the laptop into the mains means the battery's always charged when you want to go mobile.

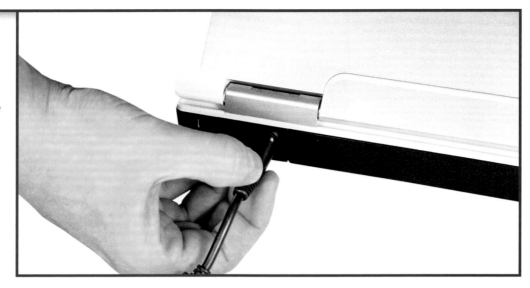

9

And here's the result: all the benefits of a desktop PC without the bulk. If you'll be using the laptop in your home office for long periods of time, it's worth putting the machine on a laptop stand: this raises the top of the screen to a better height and can help reduce neck strain.

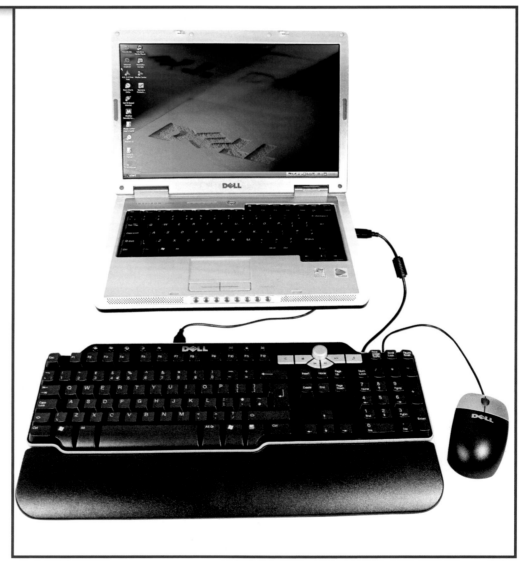

PART 2
Staying comfortable when you're out and about

Laptop stands and external keyboards are all well and good when you're at home or in the office, but of course the whole point of laptop computers is their portability. That means you can work on the train, on a plane or in a motorway service station, but it's fair to say that all these places are ergonomic disaster areas: planes are hardly comfortable and offer limited seating options; tables on trains are usually designed in such a way that they're too high for typing and too low to avoid eye strain; and motorway service stations are hardly renowned for their comfort. If you have to use your laptop in these environments, make sure the laptop you buy is fit for the purpose. For example, unless you'll be flying first class, the seats on a long-haul flight don't give you enough room to open and use a laptop with a 17 inch screen. If you plan to do a lot of computing while on board planes, small is beautiful.

No matter where you work or what kind of laptop you have, breaks are essential – if you're using the laptop for long periods, make sure you take a fifteen-minute break every hour. That doesn't mean you should stop working; just get away from the computer and do something else.

PART 2

Using your laptop with an external monitor

Most laptops can be used with an external display, so for example you could connect a flat panel monitor when you're in the office, or use the laptop as part of a twin-screen setup with the laptop showing one lot of programs and an external monitor showing another lot of programs.

Most laptops have a VGA connector that you can use to connect a display, but it's important to note that they don't all support dual-screen displays: many machines, particularly budget machines, use a technique called 'mirroring' instead. That means that what appears on the laptop screen is duplicated on the external display, but you can't display one thing on the laptop and a different thing on the external monitor. Your laptop's manual will tell you whether your machine supports dual displays or just mirroring.

Even if your laptop doesn't support dual displays, it might still be worth connecting an external monitor: while laptop screens are rarely larger than 15 inches on mid-range models and 17 inches on the really expensive ones, you could hook up a 19, 20, 26 or even 30-inch flat panel. That means you could have a laptop with a 10-inch or 12-inch screen for maximum portability and battery life, but as soon as you return to your office, you have all the benefits of a much bigger monitor.

Connecting an external display works in exactly the same way as it does with a desktop PC: simply connect the VGA cable to the VGA port on your laptop and that's it. Not all laptops have VGA connectors, though and some machines such as Apple's MacBook Pro use a more modern type of connector called a DVI connector. If your display doesn't support DVI you'll need to invest in a DVI to VGA connector, which enables you to connect a VGA cable to your laptop's DVI port.

When you connect an external display, your laptop should recognise it immediately and begin displaying the screen on the external monitor. If your laptop doesn't support a twin-screen setup it can be distracting to see the same thing on two screens, but you'll find that most machines have a function key on the keyboard that you can use to switch off the laptop screen altogether.

PART 2

Using your laptop with a projector

If you'll be connecting your laptop to a projector – for example, because you're delivering a presentation – then it's no different from connecting an external monitor, provided you have the right cable. That means you need to know the kind of connectors your laptop has and you also need to know what kind of connectors the projector has. Some projectors take the same VGA cables that monitors use, so if your laptop has a VGA port it's just a matter of running a VGA cable to the projector. If you have a DVI port instead, you can use a DVI to VGA adapter and once again, run a VGA cable to the connector.

Besides or instead of VGA connectors, many projectors accept S-Video or Composite Video connections – and many laptops have either S-Video or Composite Video plugs too. Always check these details out in advance and bring the appropriate cables and any necessary adapters – don't assume that the venue will have the cables you need or that if it does have the cables, they'll still be in working order. Cables can and do break.

TECHIE CORNER

Why closing a laptop lid can be dangerous
In the photograph opposite, we've connected an external display and then closed the laptop lid completely, but that's not always a good idea. Running in 'clamshell mode', as it's called, is fine for some machines but not for others. For example, it's okay to use an Apple PowerBook in clamshell mode but it's a bad idea to do the same with an Apple iBook. In extreme cases, running a laptop in clamshell mode could cause the machine to overheat, damaging its circuits or its screen.

The culprit is heat. Because laptops cram a lot of components into a very small space, they often get very hot – and they don't have room for the giant cooling fans you'll find in desktop computers. In some cases, laptops are designed in such a way that excess heat escapes by way of the keyboard. If you use them with the lid closed, the excess heat can no longer escape. If you're unlucky, that could mean a cooked computer – and if the machine isn't supposed to run in clamshell mode, you won't be able to get it fixed under warranty. That's why you should always check with the manufacturer: it only takes a moment to check and it could save you from killing your computer.

PART 2 Power management

Because every laptop has a battery, it's designed to offer a compromise between performance and battery life. You can tweak these settings, which is a good idea even if your laptop will never leave its desk: if you don't, you might not be getting the performance it's capable of delivering. That's because by default your laptop will be set to a 'balanced' power plan, which sacrifices some performance in the name of better energy efficiency.

Power modes

Whether you have a Windows or an Apple laptop, you'll typically have a choice of three power modes. Those modes will have different names depending on the operating system you use, but they're usually in the form of Performance, Energy Saver and Balanced. The first option, Performance, turns everything on and uses the full power of your processor and if you're running on battery power it'll give you the shortest battery life. Energy Saver reduces your performance and turns off inessential features, so your computer runs slightly more slowly but gets much longer battery life. As you might expect, Balanced offers a compromise between the two settings – so while you don't get full performance, you don't get mercilessly short battery life either. You'll find that your laptop automatically switches modes when you connect it to the mains, so when you're on battery power it'll change to Energy Saver mode and when you plug it into the mains you'll move into Performance or Balanced mode.

You can change the power-saving mode easily and you can also change the settings for each mode. Let's look at how to do this on a PC laptop running Windows Vista first and then we'll see how to achieve the same thing on a Mac.

It's worth noting that many laptop manufacturers also provide their own energy saving software, which provides additional features that aren't covered here.

Power management in Windows Vista

Windows Vista includes a new tool called the Windows Mobility Center and this provides quick access to all the power management and power-saving modes you'll ever need. Here's how to use it.

1

Right-click on the battery icon in the System Tray and select Windows Mobility Center. You'll see the screen shown here, which provides instant access to key power-saving features.

2

Wireless networking is a notorious drain on battery life, so use Windows Mobility Center to switch off your wireless card when you don't need it.

3

For maximum battery life, click the battery icon in Windows Mobility Center, select Power Saver, click Change Plan Settings and then choose Change Advanced Power Settings. You can now specify power management options for almost anything including your PC's processor.

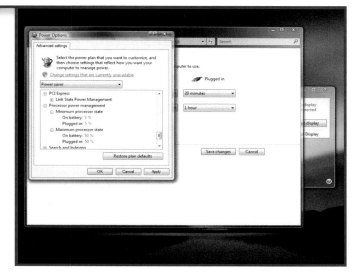

4

When this balloon pops up, it's time to swap batteries or find a power socket: while there's still a few minutes before your system hibernates to protect your data, it's a good idea to save and shut down now.

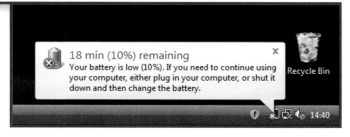

5

If you're still working when you see this message, it's time to panic: there's hardly any battery power left and your system will die without further warning in a matter of seconds, potentially taking your work with it.

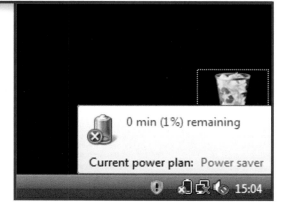

Power management on Apple laptops

As we'll discover, power management on Macs isn't much different from power management on PCs. Here's how to tweak your Mac's power settings.

1

Click on the Apple icon at the very top left of the screen and then select System Preferences. You should now see the dialog box shown in our screenshot.

2

Click on the Energy Saver icon – it looks like a lightbulb – and the dialog box will show you the selected options. In this screenshot, our Mac is plugged into the mains, so the first drop-down says Settings For Power Adapter. Click on Show Details to see more.

3

As you can see, you can adjust when the computer should go to sleep and when the screen should be switched off. If you wish, you can use the Schedule button at the bottom right of this dialog to make your Mac switch itself on and off at specific times.

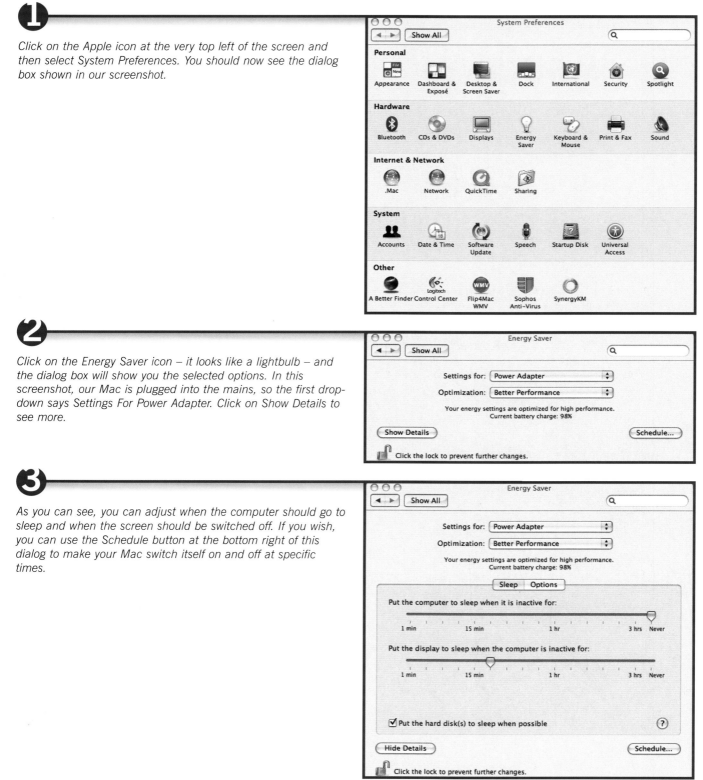

4

To change the settings for battery power, click on Settings For and select Battery. You can now choose between Normal (which balances performance with battery life), Better Performance and Better Battery Life and you can use the sliders to adjust the settings for when the system should go to sleep.

5

Click on the Options button halfway down the dialog box and you'll see three additional options, all of which will be checked if you've selected the Better Battery Life option: the first option automatically reduces the display brightness when you're running on battery power; the second option automatically dims the display before putting the screen to sleep; and the third option enables or disables the battery power icon in the status bar at the top of your Mac's screen.

6

If you've enabled the battery status icon, clicking on it provides quick access to key information and features. The first thing you'll see is how much life you've got left in hours and you can then use the Show option to decide what the battery icon should display: a battery icon that shows how full the battery is, the battery time remaining, or the percentage battery charge remaining. You can also use this menu to change power-saving mode or open the Energy Saver dialog box we've already looked at.

Getting the longest possible battery life

Besides changing the power-saving modes, you can improve battery life with a few additional steps. First, disconnect any unnecessary peripherals – do you really need that USB lava lamp? – because while they don't take huge whacks of power, every little helps. Disable wireless networking or Bluetooth if you aren't using them, because they're notorious battery hogs and reduce your display's brightness. Close any running programs you don't need, disable eye candy such as on-screen clocks, animations or photo galleries and use MP3 music files instead of CDs (or better still, don't listen to music at all). The more you get your PC to do, the more quickly you'll drain its battery.

Sleeping, suspending and hibernation

Besides switching your laptop on or off, you can make it go to sleep. This is a special low-power mode that works like the standby on a television, so the second you hit the power button or press a key your laptop bursts into life and enables you to pick up from where you left off. If you're running in Power Saver mode, your laptop will automatically sleep after a specified interval or you can make it sleep at any time by closing the laptop lid. On some laptops, simply lifting the lid again will wake the laptop up but on others you'll need to press a key or the power button to rouse your computer from its sleep.

Sleep mode is great for short-term power saving, such as when you're taking a tea break. However, if you want to shut down your laptop but pick up from where you left off the second you hit a button, hibernation is for you. This is a kind of deep sleep mode. When you choose Hibernate, your laptop saves all your work to disk; when you switch your laptop back on again, it loads the data from disk and picks up exactly where you left off. That means it takes longer to enter Hibernation mode and resume from it, but it's worth it: it uses even less power than Sleep mode.

Besides hibernating when you tell it to, your laptop will automatically hibernate when it detects that your battery is almost entirely out of juice. However, don't rely on this feature: when you're running on batteries, always save your work regularly to prevent disaster.

If you're running Windows Vista, you can change the behaviour of the laptop lid and the on/off switch in Control Panel by clicking Start > Control Panel > System and Maintenance > Power Options and then clicking on Choose What Closing The Lid Does. You can specify whether closing your laptop lid makes your computer sleep, hibernate or shut down altogether.

TECHIE CORNER

Get the best from your battery
Laptop batteries are designed to be charged and used, charged and used, charged and used again, so if your machine spends its days plugged into the mains it's a very good idea to run on battery power every few weeks. If your battery isn't regularly discharged and it's a nickel cadmium (NiCad) battery (common in older laptops), it can develop 'battery memory', which means it thinks it has a full charge when it doesn't – so when you do need to run on battery power, its life could be measured in minutes rather than hours. You don't need to do anything special to avoid battery memory – just unplug it from the mains once a month and don't plug it back in until there's hardly any battery power left.

PART ② Mobile multimedia

All work and no play makes Jack a dull boy, but the good news is that almost every laptop is as happy keeping you entertained as it is keeping tabs on business documents. If your laptop has a DVD drive – most do – then you can use it as a portable DVD player or CD jukebox and if the drive is a burner as well as a player you can even make your own discs such as compilation CDs or home-movie DVDs.

Play time

Playing discs is simple: to watch a DVD, it's just a matter of putting the disc in the drive and waiting a few seconds for your laptop's DVD player to launch. Both Apple and Windows machines come with all the software you need, so Mac OS X includes Apple's DVD Player software while Windows Vista plays movies in Windows Media Player (or Windows Media Center if you have the Home Premium or Ultimate edition of Windows Vista). Watching DVDs does use a fair bit of battery power, but even the humblest laptop should have enough battery life to play a film from start to finish without recharging – provided it's fully charged to start with and you turn off battery hogs such as Bluetooth and wireless networking, of course.

The same applies to music CDs – on a Mac, iTunes will open when you insert a CD; on a Windows laptop, you'll get Windows Media Player or Windows Media Center – but there's one crucial difference: unlike DVDs, which you can't legally copy to your hard disk, you can easily copy music CDs to your computer using a process called 'ripping'. This is a good idea for three reasons. First of all, playing music from your hard disk is less of a battery hog than playing the original CD; second, you can easily create custom playlists that choose the best tracks from your music library; and third, copying discs to your computer means you don't need to carry lots of CDs around with you when you travel.

Ripping music CDs with Windows Media Player

In this walkthrough, we'll be using the Windows Vista version of Windows Media Player, but the process is identical on Windows XP.

1

If this is the first time you've put a music CD into your PC, you'll see this AutoPlay message. If the 'Always do this' option is checked, whichever option you choose will be the default in future. As we want to store our CDs on our PC we'll keep it checked and then click on Rip Music from CD.

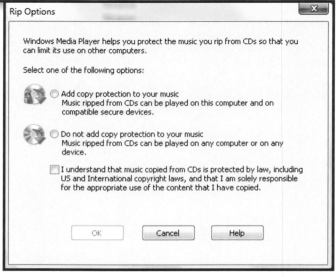

2

Microsoft is very keen for you to add copy protection to your music. There's no good reason that you should do this, so make sure the 'Do not add' option is selected before continuing. You'll need to click the box next to 'I understand' too.

3

Windows Media Player will now detect the CD in your drive and start to rip it – but we don't want to do that just yet, because by default it uses Windows Media format instead of MP3 and it uses a fairly low quality setting. Click on Stop Rip at the bottom corner of the screen and then move the mouse to the toolbar at the top of the window. Click on the arrow immediately below 'Rip' and change the Format option to MP3. We're doing this because Windows Media files don't work on all music devices, whereas MP3s work on almost anything – so if you decide to transfer a song to an iPod or mobile phone in the future, you'll be able to do it without having to convert any files.

4

From the same menu, click on the Bit Rate option. It's set to 128kbps, which delivers very small files but the sound quality isn't up to much. We'd recommend 192kbps, which increases the size of each file very slightly but offers much better audio quality.

5

Now we've changed the settings to the right format and quality, we can click on Start Rip to begin the ripping progress. As you can see Windows Media Player has automatically downloaded the album artwork and track information from the internet.

There's only one problem with the track information: it's completely wrong. This happens occasionally because US and UK CDs often have different songs on them and music software tends to assume everybody's in the United States. First of all we need to change the artist details for tracks 1, 8 and 13.

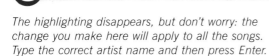

Before we change the information, we need to change it in the right place – and that means we need to amend the files in our music library. To do this click on Library at the left of the window and then use the Artist or Album links to find the CD you've just ripped. Double-click on it and you should now see the track listing.

The first thing we'll change is the artist information, which should be the same for every track. There's a quick way to do this: select all the songs, right-click and choose Edit.

The highlighting disappears, but don't worry: the change you make here will apply to all the songs. Type the correct artist name and then press Enter.

9

And here's the result: the blue highlighting has reappeared and, as you can see, all the songs now contain the correct artist information. Now to fix the song titles themselves.

10

Unfortunately there's no quick way to fix individual song titles, so we need to do it manually. To change a track name, click on the name, click again and then type the correct information. Repeat the process for any other tracks that are wrongly named.

11

And here's the final result: our freshly-ripped CD finally has the correct information. The good news is that such mistakes are very uncommon and in most cases you'll find that Windows Media Player automatically downloads the correct information. However, sometimes it can't identify a CD at all, so you need to use Windows Media Player's internet search features.

12

If Windows Media Player can't recognise a disc, you'll see a blank CD icon with Unknown Album and Unknown Artist displayed instead of the usual artwork and title information. To fix this, right-click and choose Find Album Information. You should now see the screen here, which enables you to search by artist name or album name. Alternatively you can enter the track information manually. We'll search by artist.

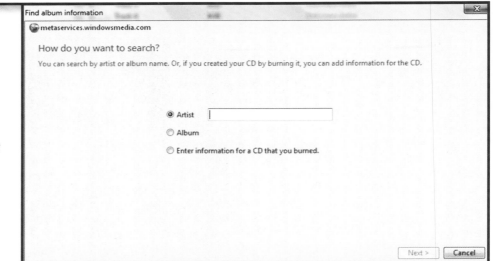

13

As you can see, Windows Media Player has found three possible matches for our search. If the program's got it wrong, select 'The artist I'm looking for is not here' and search again or enter the information manually. If Media Player has found the correct artist, as it has here, click on that artist and then click on Next.

14

Once you've chosen the artist you'll now be given a choice of album. If the correct option is on screen, simply select it and click on Next to download the artwork and track information. If the album you're looking for isn't available, choose 'The album I'm looking for is not here' to enter the information manually. Once again, such situations are relatively rare and Windows Media Player does a good job of identifying new releases and old favourites, so you won't need to use this feature very often.

Ripping music CDs with iTunes

On the face of it, Apple's iTunes does the same job as Windows Media Player, but it offers two crucial things that Windows Media Player doesn't: it's the only music software that works with Apple's iPod, which means it's a must-have if you want to transfer tracks to an iPod; and it's the only music software that works with the iTunes Music Store, the world's most popular digital download shop. That's because iTunes isn't just a music player – it's the door to a download shop that sells music, audiobooks and even movies. More of that in a moment, but first let's look at how iTunes can rip CDs and organise your tracks.

iTunes comes pre-installed on every Mac, but if you want to run it on a Windows PC you'll need to download it and install it first. The download is free and you'll find the most up-to-date version at **www.apple.com/itunes**. In this tutorial we'll use the Mac version, but the Windows version is identical.

Launch iTunes by clicking on the icon in the OS X dock (or, on Windows, by clicking on the desktop icon or running it from Start > All Programs). If this is the first time you've run the program you'll need to accept a licence agreement and tell iTunes what country you're in. Once you've done this the program will load and you'll see the iTunes Store, which will try to sell you things. We'll come back to the store in a moment.

In the menu bar, click on iTunes > Preferences (on the PC this option will be under the Tools menu). You'll now see a range of options such as text size, whether iTunes should automatically download album artwork and so on. We want to change the CD ripping settings, so click on the icon at the top labelled Advanced.

3

You'll see a number of options here. Make sure Keep iTunes Music Folder Organised is selected and that Copy Files to iTunes Music Folder is also ticked – this keeps your music organised on your PC and makes life easier in the long term – and then click on the tab labelled Importing.

Advanced

General | Podcasts | Playback | Sharing | Apple TV | Store | Advanced | Parental

General | Importing | Burning

iTunes Music folder location

Macintosh HD:Users:gary:Music:iTunes:iTunes Music: Change...   Reset

☑ Keep iTunes Music folder organized
Places files into album and artist folders, and names the files based on the disc number, track number, and the song title.

☑ Copy files to iTunes Music folder when adding to library

Use iTunes for Internet music playback   Set

Streaming Buffer Size: Medium

☑ Look for remote speakers connected with AirTunes
☐ Disable iTunes volume control for remote speakers
☐ Allow iTunes control from remote speakers

☐ Keep MiniPlayer on top of all other windows

Visualizer Size: Large
☐ Display visualizer full screen

Cancel   OK

4

There are several key options here. The first one, On CD Insert, tells iTunes what to do when you insert a CD. Make sure it's set to Import CD, so that iTunes expects to copy a disc rather than just play it. Now, look at the Import Using drop-down. There are several options here: AIFF, which creates full-quality copies but generates massive files; AAC, which is the iPod's favourite format and offers a good trade-off between quality and file size; Apple Lossless, which is almost as high quality as AIFF but without the really large file sizes; MP3, which is the industry standard format for digital music; and last but not least, WAV, which is useful if you'll be sharing full-quality tracks with Windows PCs.

So which one should you choose? We'd recommend MP3. It's not the best format ever invented but, crucially, it works on almost anything; for example, if you decide to transfer music to your mobile phone it's likely to support MP3 but not the other formats. Provided you go for the right quality settings – which we'll do in the next step – the sound quality is almost indistinguishable from CD, but the file sizes won't be so big that a single album will fill your hard disk.

Advanced

General | Podcasts | Playback | Sharing | Apple TV | Store | Advanced | Parental

General | Importing | Burning

On CD Insert: Import CD

Import Using: MP3 Encoder

Setting: Custom...

Details

96 kbps (mono)/192 kbps (stereo), VBR (Highest quality), joint stereo, optimized for MMX/SSE, using MP.

☐ Play songs while importing or converting
☑ Automatically retrieve CD track names from Internet
☑ Create file names with track number
☐ Use error correction when reading Audio CDs
Use this option if you experience problems with the audio quality from Audio CDs. This may reduce the speed of importing.

Note: These settings do not apply to songs downloaded from the iTunes Store.

Cancel   OK

MP3 Encoder

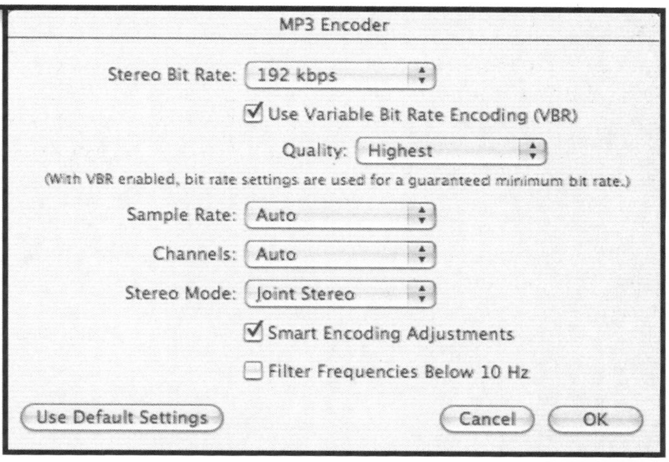

Make sure MP3 Encoder is selected and then click on the Setting drop-down immediately below it. This gives you four options: good quality, high quality, higher quality and custom. Click on Custom and then change Stereo Bit Rate to 192kbps, check the box marked Use Variable Bit Rate Encoding (VBR) and set the Quality drop-down to Highest.

What does all that mean? Those three options tell iTunes that you want your songs ripped at a quality rate that doesn't drop below 192kbps, which is indistinguishable from CD quality on normal music equipment. Selecting VBR and the Highest quality setting means that if iTunes thinks a song needs a bitrate of more than 192kbps, it'll use it. In plain English, you've told iTunes to make sure your music sounds good without creating massive digital files. Once you've done this, click OK and OK again to return to the main iTunes window.

Stereo Bit Rate:	192 kbps

☑ Use Variable Bit Rate Encoding (VBR)

Quality: Highest

(With VBR enabled, bit rate settings are used for a guaranteed minimum bit rate.)

Sample Rate: Auto

Channels: Auto

Stereo Mode: Joint Stereo

☑ Smart Encoding Adjustments

☐ Filter Frequencies Below 10 Hz

(Use Default Settings) (Cancel) (OK)

That's iTunes' ripping settings taken care of and you won't need to change them again. Now it's just a matter of putting a CD into the drive and waiting a few seconds. If you're connected to the internet iTunes will automatically detect the CD and fill in the artist name and song names and if you click on the Import CD button at the bottom right of the screen it'll start to copy the CD to your computer. The whole process should only take a few minutes and a green tick will appear at the left of each track once it's been successfully copied.

7

Once your CD has been imported, you can eject it. To see your new songs, use the navigation links at the left of the screen to click on Music (it should be immediately under the word Library at the top left of the iTunes window). You should now see your copied tracks and, if iTunes has been able to find the artwork on the internet, you should see the album cover too. To play a song, just double-click on it.

iTunes playlists work in much the same way as Windows Media Player ones. Click on the plus arrow at the very bottom left of the window to create a new playlist, give it a name and then simply drag songs from the main window over your playlist. To listen to a playlist, click on it and click on the play button. To play the songs in a random order, click on Controls > Shuffle to shuffle the playlist. This makes iTunes play the songs randomly without rearranging the playlist itself.

8

If you're playing music through your laptop's speakers the sound might not be as good as you might like, but you can change this by clicking on View > Show Equalizer. This displays a graphic equaliser and if you click on the drop-down menu you'll see a range of presets including Small Speakers, which is designed to make iTunes sound good on even the tiniest built-in speakers. You can also customise the graphic equaliser to suit your own preferences: each slider represents a frequency band, with the lowest frequency at the very left of the equaliser and the highest at the very right. Moving a slider up boosts that frequency and moving it down reduces it.

Getting the right sound tends to involve trial and error but you'll find that you'll get the best results if your sliders resemble a slight curve. For example in this screenshot we've slightly boosted the lower and higher frequencies and slightly reduced the middle frequencies and the result is a curve that looks like a very shallow U shape. Try to resist the temptation to turn every frequency up, because the result may overload your speakers and cause unpleasant distortion in the sound.

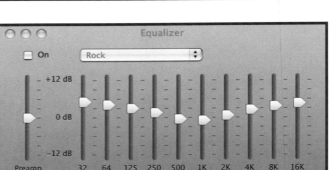

9

Besides normal playlists, iTunes has a trick up its sleeve: smart playlists. These playlists enable you to set multiple criteria such as 'songs whose genre is rock, that I haven't played in the last three months and whose artist isn't AC/DC'. To create a smart playlist, click on File > New Smart Playlist and use the drop-down fields to enter your criteria. iTunes will save the playlist and every time you run it, it will quickly scan your music library to get an up to date listing. We use smart playlists a lot, so for example we've set up playlists that only play songs we've added in the last week, last month or last three months.

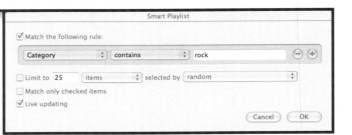

Cutting out the middleman: buying digital music online

Besides ripping CDs, your music software also enables you to buy music over the internet – and in the case of iTunes, you can buy music videos and television shows too. Before you consider doing this, though, it's important to know that your digital purchases are usually copy protected. For example, if you buy a music video from iTunes you'll only be able to play it on iTunes (or on your iPod or other Apple hardware) while if you buy a song from one of Microsoft's services in Windows Media Player, it will work in Windows Media Player but not in iTunes or on an iPod.

There is some good news, though: in mid-2007 Apple began offering digital music downloads without any copy protection whatsoever, so an unprotected track you buy from iTunes – Apple calls such tracks 'iTunes Plus' downloads – will play in Windows Media Player and will work on almost any MP3 player instead of just the iPod. However, at the time of writing the overwhelming majority of digital downloads are still protected, so make sure you know what the limits are before parting with any money.

It's also important to realise that when you buy a digital download, it's up to you to look after it – so if you suffer a hard disk crash and lose all your music, you probably won't be able to re-download the songs you've bought. If you'll be buying a lot of tunes online we'd strongly recommend regular backups to CD or even better, to an external hard disk. Check out Appendix 1 for everything you need to know about backing up crucial files.

Region codes: what they are and why they matter

The first time you play a movie DVD on your laptop, your DVD software will display a message about region codes and ask you to choose which region you want to use. It's important to think carefully here, because while you can change the region code of your drive you can only do it five times before the region code is set permanently. So what are these codes and why should you care?

When DVDs were launched, the film industry divided the world into six regions – the US and Canada is one region, Europe is another region, and so on. DVDs designed for one region will not work on DVD players set to play discs from another region, so for example a US or Canadian DVD is Region 1 and won't play on a DVD player set to Region 2, which is Europe; a US DVD player set to Region 1 won't play Region 2 discs and so on.

For most European laptop owners, the region you'll use will be Region 2, because you'll be buying your DVDs in Europe. If you're a keen importer, though (some films are only available on DVD in the US or in Japan, or come out much earlier in one region than in another; others are simply cheaper if you buy from the US), you might want to set your DVD drive to the region you're importing from rather than the one in which you live. For example, current exchange rates mean that buying discs from the US is considerably cheaper than buying the same discs in the UK – but if your laptop is permanently set to Region 2 you won't be able to play them.

PART 2

Ten terrific laptop add-ons

A few well-chosen extras can make your laptop even more useful. Of all the add-ons we've tried and tested, these are our ten favourites.

1 Wireless network card
If your laptop doesn't have wireless networking built-in, you can add wireless to it with a PC card or USB Wi-Fi adapter. Basic adapters can be as cheap as £10.

2 USB headset
Not only does a USB headset enable you to listen to DVDs or music on planes without annoying other passengers, but you can also use it to make free internet phone calls using software such as Skype (**www.skype.com**) and, if you have Windows Vista, you can control your computer and dictate documents using your voice.

3 External mouse
Whether your laptop has a trackpad, a weird wiggly joystick thing or some other mouse replacement, it's not as good or as comfortable to use as a proper mouse. USB mice cost pennies these days and even the really good ones are extremely cheap.

4 Laptop stand
We love laptop stands. They put the screen at a decent height, enable air to flow around your laptop's vents and keep your desk nice and tidy. They're cheap, too.

A laptop stand puts your computer at a more comfortable height and improves airflow around the cooling vents – although of course you'll need a separate keyboard and mouse too.

TECHIE CORNER

Too many connections!
Running out of USB sockets? A hub will help.
Whether you're connecting a keyboard or a printer you'll need to plug it into a spare USB port. That's fine with a desktop PC, where it's not unusual to have four, six or even eight USB ports, but if you use a laptop you're unlikely to have more than two USB ports. So what happens when you need to connect three, four or even more USB devices? There are two ways to deal with the problem. Many keyboards and even some monitors come with extra USB ports built in. If you have a USB keyboard, you'll often find that it has two additional USB sockets on the back. Alternatively you could invest in a USB hub. Hubs are simple and cheap bits of hardware that work like four-way electrical sockets: you plug the hub into a USB port on your computer and it gives you four or more USB sockets for your other hardware.
It's worth noting that some USB peripherals such as PocketPC cradles, wireless keyboards, USB wireless network adapters and so on need quite a lot of power, so while they'll work happily if you plug them directly into your computer they can't get enough power when they're sharing a hub with several other devices. You can get round this too, though: you can buy USB hubs that come with a power supply, which ensures that the hub delivers enough power for the most demanding peripherals.

5 Spare battery

No matter how good your laptop, its battery will run out after a few hours. A spare battery is an excellent idea if you don't want to lose power at a crucial moment – but remember to keep it charged!

6 Speakers

In almost every case, laptop speakers are rubbish for serious music listening – but your laptop will have a headphone socket that you can use to connect a decent set of speakers when you're at home. It makes a big difference to digital music.

7 External hard disk

External hard disks massively increase the amount of storage available to you and they're great for fast and reliable system backups too. Prices have plummeted in recent years and it's possible to get hundreds of gigabytes of storage space for less than £100.

8 Memory card reader

These days all kinds of devices store data on memory cards. For example, your phone might store music on a card or your digital camera might save its photos. Inevitably, every device uses a different kind of card, so a multi-card reader means you can simply pop the card into the reader and transfer files without playing hunt the cable. Some laptops have multi-card readers built in.

9 Ethernet cable

While wireless internet access is becoming more widespread, you'll often find that the only way to get online in hotel rooms is to connect an Ethernet cable to the supplied wall socket. The cable comes in handy even if wireless access is also available – if the wireless signal is patchy you'll get a more reliable connection with the cable. At home or at work, you can also use the cable to create a quick network or to connect your computer to your wireless router if your wireless network stops working.

10 USB adapter kit

If you're travelling, less is more – and a USB adapter kit means you can leave your USB cable collection at home. It's a single USB cable with three or five different connectors for different kinds of USB ports, so for example you can hook it to your laptop and then use the adapters to connect and in many cases charge your mobile phone, your digital camera or other bits of electronics kit without having to lug around a separate cable for each one.

TECHIE CORNER

Wireless wonders

One of the minor irritations about computer equipment is that the more devices you have, the more your home office resembles Spaghetti Junction. However, a growing number of devices enable you to connect peripherals without wires and you can even get wireless keyboards and mice.

Wireless keyboards and mice use one of two technologies: Bluetooth, which is Apple's preferred option for its wireless equipment, and radio waves, which are used by manufacturers such as Logitech. Bluetooth devices only work with Bluetooth-enabled computers such as Apple's iMacs, while radio-wave cordless devices use a receiver that plugs into a spare USB port. Although Bluetooth is less prone to interference from other devices than radio waves, we've found that there's little practical difference between Bluetooth and radio keyboards: the choice really depends on whether your computer has Bluetooth and on which particular keyboard and mouse you like the look of. We'll explore Bluetooth in more detail in Part 3.

Cordless keyboards and mice such as Logitech's Cordless Desktop can help reduce cable clutter.

PART 3 Connectivity

Laptops make great tools by themselves, but they become even more useful when you take advantage of their connectivity options. Wireless networking means you can get online from hotel rooms, motorway service stations, libraries and coffee shops, while Bluetooth technology can transfer data between your laptop and your mobile phone. And of course, laptops can connect to other computers too. In this section, we discover what connectivity features your laptop has and how you can make the most of them.

CONNECTIVITY

Internet everywhere

One of the most important features of any laptop is its ability to connect to the internet. You can do this in two ways: by connecting an Ethernet cable (a common way to get online in hotel rooms) or by connecting to a wireless network. Wireless networks are springing up everywhere, but they usually cost money – although many mobile phone companies now offer a bundle of wireless minutes so you can surf for free when you're out and about. If not, you'll need to sign up with a wireless provider such as BT OpenZone (**www.btopenzone.com**) or T-Mobile (**www.t-mobile.co.uk**) to use their hotspots.

A hotspot is simply a location where wireless internet access is available and you'll find them in branches of McDonald's, in airport terminals, in train stations, in business centres and anywhere else laptop users might want to get online. If you don't have an account with a hotspot provider there is a pay-as-you-go option, but it isn't cheap: as of Summer 2007 you pay around £6 for an hour's access. If you think you'll be using wireless networks a lot, a monthly package will save you a packet – particularly if you use hotspots instead of hotel room connections, which tend to be very slow and extremely expensive.

There's a third option: connecting to the internet by way of the mobile phone network. Doing so used to be extremely expensive and irritatingly slow, but things have improved dramatically in recent years – although it's still one of the most expensive ways to get online.

In this chapter we'll cover all these options. We'll show you how to connect to a wireless hotspot, how to create your own wireless network at home or at work and how to use other options such as Bluetooth and mobile phone data cards.

PART ③ Connecting to a wireless network

All wireless networks work in much the same way so, provided you have a wireless card or a laptop with built-in wireless networking, it's just a matter of finding the network and connecting to it.

Windows Vista

❶

If your wireless adapter is switched on and you're within range of a wireless network, Windows Vista will find the network for you and pop up this message above the taskbar.

❷

Right-click over the network icon (two PC screens with a globe) and you'll see a list of available options. Click on 'Connect to a network' to see what wireless networks are available.

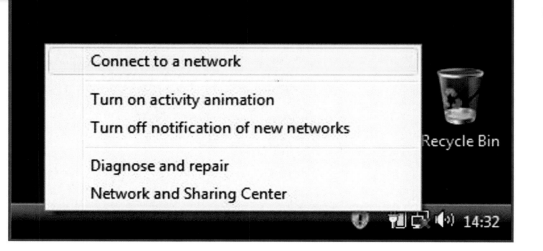

3

We're within range of two networks: our own network (the one with the hilarious name) and our next-door neighbours' network. Windows Vista shows whether the available networks are security protected and it also tells you how strong their signals are. To choose a network, click on it and then click Connect.

4

Windows Vista will now attempt to connect to your chosen wireless network. If it's password-protected you'll be asked for the password at this stage; if you don't know the password, you won't be able to connect.

5

Time for a new pop-up, this time telling us that we've successfully connected to our chosen network and we have both local access – to other machines on the network – and internet access. If you're connecting to a paid-for wireless network, such as the ones you'll find in motorway service stations, hotels and airports, when you use your web browser you'll be automatically taken to a login page which asks for your username and password. If you don't have either, you'll find a sign-up page that asks for your credit card (or, in the case of a hotel, asks you to confirm that you want to charge the internet access to your room). You won't be able to access any normal sites or use your email program until you've logged in.

Mac OS X

Now we'll do the same thing on a Mac. As you'll see, the process is nice and simple.

①

Apple's approach to wireless is very similar to Microsoft's, but instead of an icon at the bottom right of the screen it's the radio-wave icon at the top right. Click on that and you'll see this window. The first step is to turn on AirPort (Apple's name for Wi-Fi) if it isn't on already. Once you've done that, you'll see a list of available wireless networks, so for example in this screenshot you'll see that we're within range of a network with the daft name of 'teh intarwebs'. The tick box means we're connected. To connect to a different network just click its name or click on Other.

②

If your chosen network is password protected you'll see this screen when you try to connect to it. You'll need to know which kind of password to use – in this screenshot, our network needs a WEP password, which is the most basic kind of wireless security. Once you've chosen the correct password type and entered the password, clicking OK connects you.

PART Setting up a broadband internet connection

So far we've discovered how to connect to existing wireless networks. Now, we'll discover how you can create, configure and use a wireless network at home or in the office. In this tutorial, we use a wireless broadband router, which enables us to share our connection wirelessly with other computers. First of all we discover how to establish an internet connection and connect computers by way of Ethernet cables – the fastest and easiest option for a home network – and then we find out how to share our broadband connection wirelessly.

Making the physical connections

The first step is to connect the broadband cable, which looks like a telephone cable, to the back of the router. If you're using ADSL broadband, connect the other end to a microfilter – a box that splits your phone line into two connections, one for the phone and the other for the broadband – which plugs into the phone socket. Without a microfilter you'll lose your internet connection whenever you use the phone.

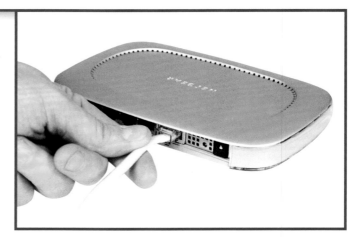

Now, you can connect your PC. We've already connected an Ethernet cable to the back of the PC and it's just a matter of plugging the other end of the cable into one of the empty Ethernet ports on the back of the router.

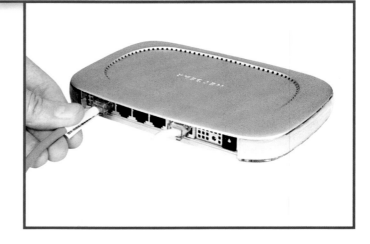

3

If you'll be sharing your broadband connection with more than one computer, you can do it with an Ethernet cable (as shown here): simply get a second cable, plug one end into the PC and plug the other end into the next available Ethernet port on the router. If you will be connecting your other devices by way of wireless, you can skip this step.

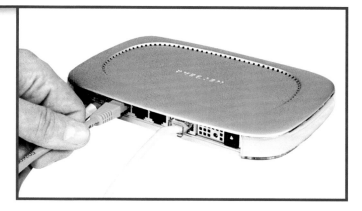

4

If you've got a third or fourth computer to connect or a networked printer, it's time for yet another Ethernet cable. Once your various computers are connected, you can connect the power cable. It's a good idea to keep the router and its various cables out of harm's way: trailing cables can be a trip hazard and a good tug on a cable could damage it, the router or whatever else the cable is connected to.

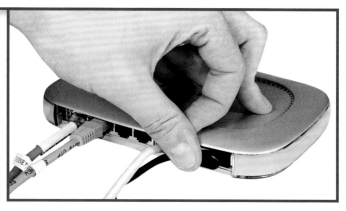

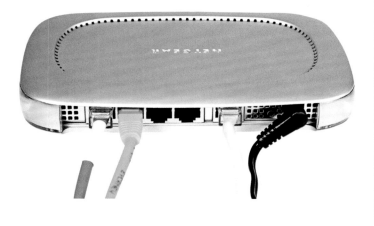

TECHIE CORNER

What is a microfilter?

With ADSL broadband, your phone and your internet connection share the same phone line – but if you connect your phone and your computer using a standard splitter plug, you'll lose your internet connection any time you make or receive a telephone call.

A microfilter prevents this from happening and ensures that your phone and your internet connection can co-exist peacefully. When you sign up for broadband your ISP will usually provide at least one such filter, but if it doesn't you can buy microfilters from any high street or online electronics shop. If you have more than one phone connected to the same line that delivers your broadband, you'll need a microfilter for each phone socket. The good news is that they aren't expensive: you can get microfilters for around £3 each.

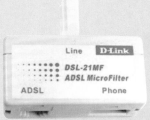

Microfilters keep your phones and broadband connection separate, so you won't lose your internet connection every time the phone rings.

Configuring a broadband router

Before you can use your router, you need to configure it. For most routers – wired or wireless – you do that by way of your Web browser. The good news is it's very quick and very easy to do, as we'll discover in this walkthrough.

1

Once you've connected your cables and plugged in the power cord, boot up your PC and open your web browser. To access the router configuration screen you'll need to type its address in your Web browser. The router manual will tell you what this address is: in this example we're using a Netgear router and the address we have to type is http://192.168.0.1

http://192.168.0.1

2

The router will ask for a user name and password. Once again, you'll find these details in the manual. With Netgear routers, the default username is 'admin' and the default password is 'password', so if you enter those details in the appropriate boxes you'll be able to access your router's control panel. Remember to change the user name and password later or anybody will be able to log in and change your settings!

Prompt

Enter username and password for "NETGEAR DG834GT" at 192.168.0.1

User Name:
admin

Password:
****

☑ Use Password Manager to remember this password.

Cancel   OK

3

The control panel looks like a typical Web page with a range of categories down the left side of the screen. The first thing we need to do is to configure the router to work with our broadband connection. You'll need your ISP's login details and connection settings to do this, so make sure you've got them handy before attempting this step. Once you've got the necessary details to hand, click on Basic Settings on the left of the screen.

• **Setup Wizard**

Setup

• **Basic Settings**

• **ADSL Settings**

• **Wireless Settings**

4

Every manufacturer takes a slightly different approach, but the principles are the same: you'll be asked whether your connection requires a login (most do) and then for your username and password. You'll also be asked to specify the encapsulation type – your ISP will have given you this information – and to specify your IP and domain name server (DNS) addresses. In most cases, the correct options will be 'Get Dynamically from ISP' and 'Get Automatically from ISP'. Your ISP will have provided the necessary numbers if that isn't the case. Finally, you need to select whether network address translation (NAT) should be enabled; again, in most cases the answer is yes.

Don't worry about the various acronyms – DNS, NAT and so on. All you need to do is to ensure that the information you enter into the router control panel matches the details you've been given by your internet service provider.

Basic Settings

Does Your Internet Connection Require A Login?
- ● Yes
- ○ No

Encapsulation PPPoA (PPP over ATM)

Login bddsl-98787@bulldc
Password ********
Idle Timeout (In Minutes) 0

Internet IP Address
- ● Get Dynamically From ISP
- ○ Use Static IP Address
  IP Address . . .

Domain Name Server (DNS) Address
- ● Get Automatically From ISP
- ○ Use These DNS Servers
  Primary DNS 194 . 72 . 6 . 52
  Secondary DNS 193 . 113 . 212 . 38

NAT (Network Address Translation)
- ● Enable ○ Disable

5

Once you've entered the details, click on Apply to save them permanently. The router will now attempt to connect to your broadband connection using the details you've specified. Netgear routers display a pop-up window that provides a progress report on how it's getting on. If the information you've entered is correct, after a few seconds the pop-up window changes and displays the 'success page' shown here. You're up and running!

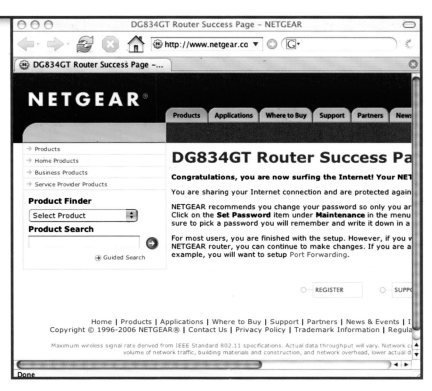

Configuring the wireless network

If you're using a wired router, you can now connect your PCs to the internet without any more changes. If you want to connect PCs to the router over a wireless connection, though, you need to specify a few more details.

1

Click on Wireless Settings and in the Name (SSID) box, choose a descriptive name for your network such as 'my home office'. Make sure that Enable Wireless Access Point and Allow Broadcast of Name (SSID) are ticked: if they aren't, then your computers won't be able to find the wireless network. These options tell the router that it should let computers connect to it and that it should broadcast a message that essentially says 'hello! I'm a wireless network and my name is "my home office"'.

Wireless Settings

Wireless Network
Name (SSID): my home office
Region: Europe
Channel: Auto
Mode: Auto 108Mbps

Wireless Access Point
☑ Enable Wireless Access Point
☑ Allow Broadcast of Name (SSID)
☐ Wireless Isolation
☐ Atheros eXtended Range (XR)

Wireless Station Access List (Setup Access List)

Security Options
○ Disable
● WEP (Wired Equivalent Privacy)
○ WPA-PSK (Wi-Fi Protected Access Pre-Shared Key)
○ WPA-802.1x

2

Now to make your wireless network secure. Click on the Wired Equivalent Privacy (WEP) button to enable the WEP security system and then choose '128 bit' from the Encryption Strength field. This makes it very difficult for people to get into your network. Now, you need to create a security key. In the Passphrase box, type any phrase you like; the router then generates a complicated password, called a 'key', such as 9588BEF5DD4... . Take a note of this number: you'll need to enter it on any computer that will use your wireless network. Click on Apply to save the settings.

WEP Security Encryption
Authentication Type: Automatic
Encryption Strength: 128 bit
WEP Key
Passphrase: (Generate)
Key 1: ● 9588BEF5DD43D922DFA7F49355
Key 2: ○ 9588BEF5DD43D922DFA7F49355
Key 3: ○ 9588BEF5DD43D922DFA7F49355
Key 4: ○ 9588BEF5DD43D922DFA7F49355

(Apply) (Cancel)

3

Whenever a wireless-enabled computer is within range of your network, it will spot 'my home network' and ask if you want to connect with it. This is where the key you wrote down in Step 2 matters: without it, you won't be able to connect to the network (this is a good thing, because it keeps other people's computers out of your network). In this screenshot, we're connecting with an Apple computer: because we've entered the correct wireless key, when we click on OK we are connected to the network.

Closed Network

Choose a security type and enter the name of the AirPort network to join with an optional password.

Network Name: my home office
Wireless Security: WEP 40/128-bit hex
Password: 9588bef5dd43d922dfa7f49355
☑ Show password

(?) (Cancel) (OK)

PART 3

Wireless security: making sense of the alphabet soup

The single best thing about wireless networks is that they work through walls. Unfortunately, the single worst thing about wireless networks is that they work through walls. As we write this, we're within range of two wireless networks: our own and our next-door neighbours'. They can't connect to our wireless network, but we can connect to theirs. That's because our wireless network is secure and theirs isn't.

It's very easy to secure a wireless network – we did it in Step 2 above – and for extra security you can even create an 'access list' of computers. That turns your wireless router into an electronic bouncer: if a computer isn't on the list, it doesn't get into your network.

There are very good reasons for securing a wireless network, although they might not be obvious. For example, while the average person doesn't have the technical know-how to hack your system and steal your important files, if your network isn't secured it's child's play for anyone within range to connect and then use your internet connection. That's bad news for two reasons: they're getting internet access that you're paying for and, more seriously, they could be up to no good. If they're caught, you could end up with the blame.

The simplest way to secure your wireless network is to password-protect it. You'd be surprised how many people don't carry out this simple step.

Choose a security type and enter the name of the AirPort network to join with an optional password.

Network Name: default

Wireless Security: WEP Password

Password:

☐ Show password

(?)   (Cancel) (OK)

Why letting other people use your net connection is a bad idea

Whenever you connect to the internet, your ISP gives you a unique address, which is the internet equivalent of a telephone number. This address, known as the IP address, is logged – so if you try to hack into the Pentagon or look at illegal content, you can be traced. Although ISPs don't spy on you they do keep logs of IP addresses and their activity and the police can compel them to hand over those logs if they believe a crime has been committed. When you use a wireless network, the IP address is assigned to your router and to any machine connected to it. That means that if someone else connects to your network, anything they do comes from your IP address.

Of course, you're a perfectly law-abiding, upstanding member of the public – but what about the people next door or people you haven't met? Although wireless networks don't extend too far, they do extend into the street – and, as a lot of companies have discovered, that means people can sit outside in their cars and take advantage of wireless internet access for dodgy purposes. In the US, a number of people have been prosecuted for doing just that.

There's another, less dramatic, reason not to share your broadband connection with other people: in most cases, your ISP's terms and conditions state that you can't share your broadband with anyone who doesn't share your building.

Securing a wireless network

In our walkthrough we used WEP to prevent unauthorised computers from joining our wireless network. However, it's not the only standard and, although all wireless equipment supports WEP, more recent hardware supports even stronger security standards. The two standards you'll see most often are Wi-Fi Protected Access Pre-Shared Key (WPA-PSK) and WPA-802.1x. But what are they?

WPA-PSK is a stronger form of security that's specifically designed for small office and home users. Although it's more secure than WEP, it works in essentially the same way: to connect to your network, computers need to support WPA-PSK security and know the correct network key. The main difference between WEP and WPA-PSK is that the latter is a bit harder for villains to break into. WPA-802.1x is tougher still, but it's really designed for big companies and is intended to be used with a computer server that checks whether computers should be allowed to connect to the network.

Creating an access list

Whether you use WEP or WPA-PSK, it's worth considering an access list that turns your router into an electronic bouncer: if your name's not on the list, you don't get in. With most wireless networks, any computer can connect as long as it knows the correct key, but for added security you can create a 'guest list' of machines. If a computer isn't on the list, it can't connect to the network – even if it has the correct key. To set up an access list, you'll need to know the Media Access Control (MAC) addresses of the computers. These are twelve-digit numbers, usually broken up by colons for easier reading. For example, the MAC address of our current computer is 00:0d:93:7e:e1:de.

Finding your MAC address is very simple, but the process is slightly different on different types of computers. Here's how to find it:

Windows PC

Connect to your wireless network and then click on the Start button. Select Run and in the dialog box that appears, type 'cmd' (without the inverted commas) and press Return. In the small black window that appears, type 'ipconfig /all' (again, without the inverted commas) and look for the bit that says Physical Address. That's your PC's MAC address.

Apple Mac

Connect to your wireless network and then open System Preferences > Network. Click on AirPort and then on the Configure button. Your Mac's MAC address will be displayed in the form 'AirPort ID: 00:0d:93:7e:e1:de' (the actual numbers will differ from computer to computer).

Windows Mobile devices

Connect to the wireless network. The specific procedure then depends on the type of Pocket PC you have, but in most cases you need to click Start > Settings > Connections and then locate the wireless network manager software – which, handily, is usually called something like Wireless Network Manager, WLAN Utility or something similar. You'll find the MAC address in the Advanced tab.

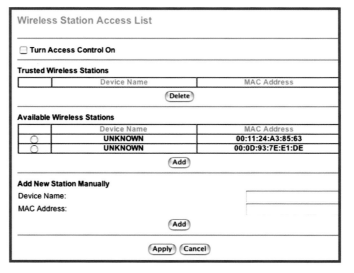

Once you've noted the MAC addresses of your computers, creating the access list is very simple. Once again we'll use a Netgear router, but other manufacturers' routers work in much the same way. Use your Web browser to open the router's control panel and then click on Wireless Settings. Now, click on the Setup Access List button.

To prevent other machines from accessing your network, simply click the Turn Access Control On button and then use Add New Station Manually to enter the details of the computers you want the router to talk to. For example, to add our laptop, we type 'Laptop' in the Device Name box and 00:0d:93:7e:e1:de in the MAC Address box.

PART ③ Wireless standards and what they mean

There are two main wireless standards: 802.11b and 802.11g. They both work in the same way but 802.11g is much faster than 802.11b and uses slightly different technology, so a wireless card that only supports the b standard won't be able to connect to a g network. However, most wireless cards now support both standards: look for products that are described as 802.11b/g and you'll be able to connect not just to your own wireless network, but to public wireless networks too.

There's a third standard, 802.11n. This is even faster than 802.11g and it uses a technology called MIMO – multiple inputs, multiple outputs – to improve signal strength and speed. However, at the time of writing, the 802.11n standard hasn't been finalised. That hasn't stopped companies selling 802.11n hardware, but beware: until the standard has been agreed by all the main players, you might find that so-called 'pre-n' hardware doesn't work properly with other firms' 802.11n products.

If that wasn't confusing enough, some manufacturers also offer their own versions of existing standards (for example, you'll see wireless products advertised as 'Super G') that offer much faster speeds than 802.11g is supposed to deliver. Such products do work, but they only work with other products that use the same technology – so if you buy a Super G router but a standard 802.11g wireless network card, you won't get any benefit from the Super G technology.

Beware 'standards' such as Super G: they're the manufacturer's own, so if you use other firms' equipment you might not get the advertised speeds.

NETGEAR

TREND MICRO

108 Mbps
2.4 GHz
802.11

Super G Wireless Router
WGT624SC
Security Edition

Free Trend Micro Home Network Security

• Protects against viruses, spyware, spam email and other Internet security threats
• Parental Controls protect your family from inappropriate Web content

NETGEAR

PART 3 Wireless speed and range

According to the blurb, 802.11b kit delivers connection speeds of 11Mbps (megabits per second) while 802.11g kit ups that to 54Mbps. That's much faster than a broadband connection, but the figures are somewhat misleading. The figures you'll see on the box are maximums and you'll never achieve them in the real world.

There are two reasons for this. The first is that the speed is shared by however many machines are connected, so if you have two computers accessing an 11Mbps connection then they get 5.5Mbps each. The speed also drops with distance – 802.11b's range is around 150 metres, but the signal strength drops dramatically long before that point, particularly if the signal has to pass through walls or other obstacles. The further you are from the wireless router, the slower your connection will be.

The second reason the quoted speeds are over-optimistic is due to 'overheads'. Some of the data transferred between a wireless device and a wireless router is about the connection – essentially the router is asking 'is anybody there?' and your computer replies 'yes, I'm over here!' That chatter is essential to establish and maintain any wireless connection, but it takes a lot of data – typically 40 to 50% of the network connection. So your 11Mbps connection drops to around 5.5Mbps before you even get started and when you connect a second PC the speed halves again to around 2.75Mbps – and it gets even slower the further away you are from the wireless router.

Does any of this matter? Yes and no. Even 2.75Mbps is fast enough for sharing a 512Kbps broadband connection, but there's not much point in spending money on a 22Mbps broadband connection if your wireless kit can't deliver it to your computer. That's why it makes sense to get the fastest wireless kit you can afford: the difference in price between 802.11b and 802.11g kit isn't dramatic, but if you're getting a fast broadband connection that you want to use with multiple computers then the faster kit is worth the extra expense.

TECHIE CORNER

Are wireless networks dangerous?
Every few weeks the newspapers report a new scare over wireless networks, suggesting that they contribute to 'electronic smog' that's really bad for our health. However, despite the lurid headlines, at the time of writing there's no suggestion that wireless networks are dangerous in any way at all – and while the papers recount the stories of people who claim to suffer debilitating effects when mobile phone or wireless networks are present, 31 different studies have found no evidence to support such claims. There's no doubt that the people are genuinely suffering from something, but wireless networks and mobile phones don't seem to be the culprits.
Should you worry? Well, it makes sense to worry about mobile phones first: they use similar electromagnetic fields to Wi-Fi, but the signals are much stronger and you don't hold your laptop next to your ear. However, once again there's no evidence so far that mobile phones are dangerous.

Other ways to connect when you're on the move

When you're out and about, you might not be anywhere near a wireless network – but you might still need to get online. You can do this by connecting through a mobile phone. Thanks to Bluetooth technology, it's easier to do this than ever before. If your laptop and your mobile phone both support Bluetooth you can quickly and easily use your mobile phone as a modem and that means you can get online anywhere you can get a mobile phone signal.

Before you use Bluetooth, though, there are a few points to consider. The first is that unless your phone connects to the super-fast 3G network, which offers broadband-style connection speeds, getting online with your mobile phone is going to be very slow. Even with 3G, fast speeds aren't guaranteed, because 3G coverage can be patchy outside cities – so if it's not available, your mobile phone will resort to the slower General Packet Radio Service (GPRS) technology. And if that's not available either, you'll end up on the Global System for Mobile Communication (GSM) network.

Most recent mobile phones support GPRS for data access, but older ones don't – and that means they use GSM. You might also find that even if you have a GPRS or 3G phone, if you're travelling abroad GSM might be the only connection technology available where you are. Does this matter? Sadly yes, because GSM is extremely slow and desperately expensive.

Why you should run away from GSM connections

With a GSM connection, the maximum data transfer speed you'll get is 14.4Kbps (9.6Kbps on older GSM networks) – and, like all maximum speeds, the real rate you'll get will be considerably slower than that. By comparison a plain old (landline) telephone modem delivers speeds of around 40Kbps, ultra-cheap broadband offers 512Kbps and standard home broadband services deliver 2048Kbps.

The other reason to avoid GSM connections is because they're desperately, terrifyingly expensive. GSM data calls are charged according to how much time you spend connected and, because of the tortoise-like speed, even downloading a few emails will take forever. No matter what you do, the clock is ticking – so if you do a quick Google search and then read the resulting webpages, you'll be paying steep data charges for every second you spend reading.

GPRS is better because you pay for the data you use, not the time you spend using it – so if you download a few emails and then spend ages reading them, you're only charged for the actual download. It doesn't matter if you read the emails in ten seconds

or two hours; you'll pay the same rate. However, once again GPRS can be expensive, although it's nowhere near as bad as GSM. If you're willing to spend a bit of time scouring the small print on your mobile phone provider's website you'll often find that they offer unlimited GPRS data packages for a reasonable monthly fee, although it's important to ensure that the plan you choose explicitly supports laptop use. Not all do.

If you don't sign up for a data plan, be careful. Charges are usually per megabyte (MB) and are added to your monthly bill. They can be an unpleasant surprise if you do a lot of web browsing. Phone companies suggest that 1MB is equivalent to around 100 web pages, but that's based on pages of one-hundredth of a megabyte apiece. Real-world pages are often much bigger; for example, the front page of **www.Telegraph.co.uk** is around one-twentieth of a megabyte. As a rule of thumb, assume that 1MB of data gives you around 25 decent web pages, one third of an MP3 music file or 30 seconds of a YouTube video. With firms charging around £2 to £3 per megabyte, the costs of browsing soon add up. If you plan to do more than the odd bit of browsing or emailing, a monthly plan will save you a great deal of money.

Of all the ways to connect, 3G is the best – because it's almost as fast as a home broadband connection. As with GPRS, data bundles are available. Vodafone, for example, offers a laptop-friendly 3G service with prices starting at around £25 per month. You don't necessarily need a mobile phone to access it, either: Vodafone offers a 3G PC Card that slides into the PC Card slot of your laptop and it also has a USB modem for laptop owners who either don't have a PC Card slot or who already have something else plugged into it. These bits of kit take the mobile phone out of the equation and connect your laptop directly to the 3G network.

No matter which kind of connection technology you plump for, beware of the word 'unlimited' in any contracts. You're encouraged to think that if you sign up for an unlimited monthly data plan you'll be able to use anything you like for as long as you like, but that isn't the case. Most unlimited mobile phone data plans have a fair use policy that specifies a maximum monthly amount of data transfer; if you exceed it, you may have to pay extra or accept restrictions on your account.

Using your mobile phone as a modem with Bluetooth

Bluetooth is a wonderful technology, delivering fast, wire-free connections between computers, phones, headsets and other handy gadgets. However, if you've ever wept with frustration after trying to persuade a Bluetooth headset to communicate with your mobile phone, you'll know it isn't always easy to set up.

In this tutorial we'll show you how we set up a Bluetooth connection between an Apple MacBook Pro and a Blackberry mobile phone, but what we can't show you are the angry faces and stomping that went on behind the scenes. The process isn't particularly difficult but mobile phone operators seem determined to make it as complicated as possible; for example, the information from our mobile phone provider (O2) took half an hour to find, required wading through dozens of pages of text and turned out to be completely and utterly wrong.

There are several key bits of information you need to provide to get connected and the only way to get that information is to get it

from your mobile phone provider. We'd strongly advise calling their helpline to get the information and staying on the line until you're sure you've been given the correct details. That way you won't do what we did and spend an entire morning in a foul mood.

Before you can configure your laptop you'll need to set up your mobile phone. It should already be configured for GPRS or 3G internet access – phones are pre-configured before they're delivered to you so you can take them out of the box, charge the battery and start using them straight away – but you'll also need to find your phone's Bluetooth settings. The location of these settings varies from phone to phone, but typically you'll find the necessary bit under System, Options, Configuration or something similar. Once you've located the Bluetooth settings you need to do two things: turn Bluetooth on and make sure it's set as 'discoverable'. That means other Bluetooth devices can 'see' your mobile phone – if your laptop can't see the phone, it can't use it.

To connect to a mobile phone we need to do two things: we need to set up Bluetooth and we need to set up the internet connection. We'll do the first one now. Click on the Apple logo at the top left of the screen and select System Preferences. Click on the Bluetooth icon.

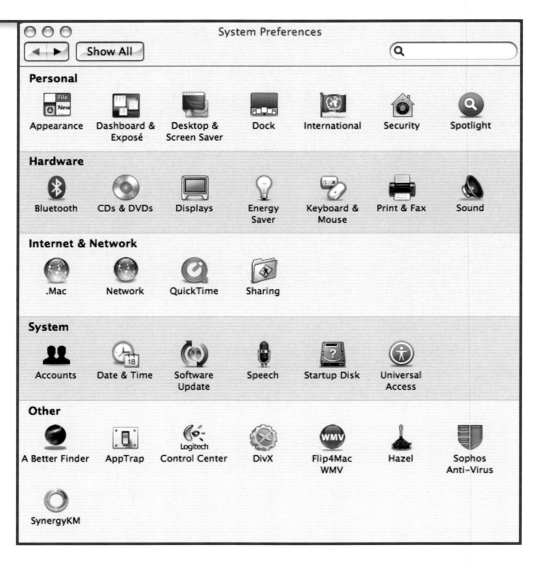

2

You'll now see the first screen in OS X's Bluetooth settings. Before we can do anything else we need to turn Bluetooth on. If the button at the right of the window says 'Turn Bluetooth On', that means it's currently switched off. Click the button to enable Bluetooth.

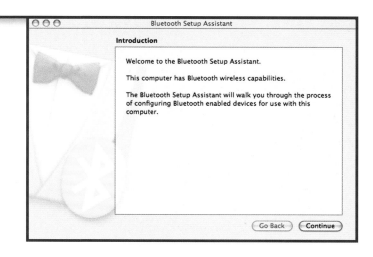

3

Click on the Devices tab and you should see the screen shown here. The laptop hasn't teamed up with any Bluetooth devices yet, so we need to click on Set Up New Device to introduce it to our mobile phone.

4

This is the Bluetooth Setup Assistant, which takes you step by step through the process of adding a new Bluetooth device. Although we'll be using it to add a mobile phone, you can add any Bluetooth-enabled device such as a wireless printer or keyboard. Click on Continue.

5

The laptop needs to know what kind of device it's going to be looking for, so make sure the Mobile Phone option is selected. Click on the Continue button.

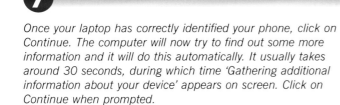

Bluetooth Setup Assistant

Select Device Type

The Bluetooth Setup Assistant sets up your Bluetooth device to work with this computer. Select the type of device you want to set up from the list. Select "Any device" if the device you want to set up is not on the list. Your device needs to be within 30 feet of your computer.

○ Mouse
○ Keyboard
⦿ Mobile phone
○ Printer
○ Headset
○ Any device

(Go Back) (Continue)

6

The laptop will now attempt to connect to your mobile phone. At this point your phone may display a message asking you whether you want to accept the connection. You need to say yes to this, or you won't be able to continue. If your mobile phone has a 'don't ask me again' option, select this before saying yes. It'll save you a lot of clicking later.

Bluetooth Setup Assistant

Bluetooth Mobile Phone Set Up

Searching for your mobile phone

When your mobile phone appears in the list, select it and click Continue. If you don't see your mobile phone in the list, make sure your mobile phone is "discoverable."

Mobile Phones
BlackBerry 8100

⟳ Searching for mobile phones – 1 found.

(Go Back) (Continue)

7

Once your laptop has correctly identified your phone, click on Continue. The computer will now try to find out some more information and it will do this automatically. It usually takes around 30 seconds, during which time 'Gathering additional information about your device' appears on screen. Click on Continue when prompted.

Bluetooth Setup Assistant

Bluetooth Mobile Phone Set Up

Gathering information about your device

The computer needs information about your device to determine how it can interact with it. This should only take a few seconds.

⟳ Gathering additional information about your device...

(Go Back) (Continue)

8

The laptop generates a pass key, which is a numerical password. Your mobile phone will ask you to enter this code and if you don't or you get it wrong then it won't let the laptop connect. It's a simple but effective security measure and you don't need to provide it every time you connect in future.

9

When you enter the correct pass key, your phone will send the laptop a quick 'everything's fine' message and you'll be taken to the next step. The first option, Use With Address Book, enables you to synchronise contacts between your mobile phone's address book and your computer one, which is handy, but the important options are the two 'Access the Internet' ones. 'Dial a specific access number' is for old-fashioned GSM connections; for GPRS or 3G phones select 'Use a direct, higher speed connection' and click Continue.

10

Now for the fun part. You need to provide a Username, Password and 'CID String' – or phone number – for your GPRS or 3G account. Every phone operator is different, so you'll need to get this information from your mobile phone company. The information you enter here is crucial: if it's incorrect, you might be able to connect to the internet by way of your phone but you'll be disconnected immediately.

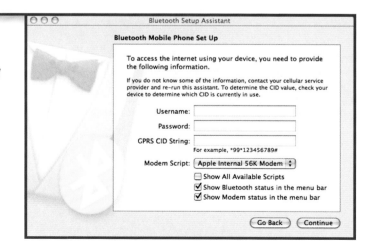

At the time of writing, this is the correct information for O2 GPRS connections: the username is 'o2web', the password is 'password' and the CID string is 'mobile.o2.co.uk'. Once you've entered that, click on Modem Script and choose the correct one for your phone. It's a huge list but if you find that your phone isn't listed, you'll need to download the appropriate script for your phone (it's usually available from your phone operator, but if not a quick Google will uncover the right one) and drop it into the Macintosh HD > Library > Modem Scripts folder on your computer before you can continue. If you do download the script, make sure it doesn't have an extension – so for example a file called 'Blackberry 8100' will work, but 'Blackberry 8100.txt' will not – and click on Show All Available Scripts so that it appears in the list.

'Congratulations!', says the computer – to which we have to answer, 'not so fast, buddy!', because while that's the Bluetooth bits set up correctly, O2's internet service requires making some changes to our laptop's internet settings too. Once again, every mobile phone operator is different and once again we'd strongly advise getting the relevant details from their helpline rather than trying to find them on the internet.

If you haven't closed System Preferences, click on it and then click Show All at the top left of the window to return to the main System Preferences menu. If you've already closed it, relaunch it by clicking on the Apple logo at the top left of your screen and selecting System Preferences. Now, click on the Network icon and you should see the screen shown here. Click on Bluetooth and then click on Configure. Don't worry if you don't have as many on-screen options as we do here; as long as there's a Bluetooth option (which there will be) everything is hunky-dory.

14

Once again we need to enter the account information for the mobile phone network connection. The Service Provider field is just a label so you can put anything you want in here, but the correct account name (the username you used for the Bluetooth connection), password and phone number (the GPRS CID from before) are essential here. Enter the correct details and then click on the PPP Options button.

	Network

○ ○ ○

◄ ► Show All

Location: Automatic ⬍

Show: Bluetooth ⬍

PPP TCP/IP Proxies Bluetooth Modem

Service Provider: O2 (Optional)

Account Name: mobileweb

Password: ••••••••

Telephone Number: mobile.o2.co.uk

Alternate Number: (Optional)

☑ Save password
Checking this box allows all users of this computer to access this Internet account without entering a password.

PPP Options...   Dial Now...

(?)

🔓 Click the lock to prevent further changes.   Assist me...   Apply Now

15

A new window pops up with various technical-sounding options. What they do doesn't really matter; what's important here is that – for O2, at least – all the boxes in the Advanced Options section of the window should be unchecked. You'll probably find that 'Send PPP echo packets' and 'Use TCP header compression' are ticked; click on them to uncheck the boxes and then click on OK.

Session Options:

☐ Connect automatically when needed

☐ Prompt every 30 minutes to maintain connection

☐ Disconnect if idle for 10 minutes

☑ Disconnect when user logs out

☑ Disconnect when switching user accounts

☑ Redial if busy

Redial 1 times

Wait 5 seconds before redialing

Advanced Options:

Terminal Script: None ⬍

☐ Send PPP echo packets

☐ Use TCP header compression

☐ Connect using a terminal window (command line)

☐ Prompt for password after dialing

☐ Use verbose logging

Cancel   OK

16

Now, click on the Bluetooth Modem button. Once again the options you select here may be different depending on your phone provider, but for O2 we need to ensure that 'Enable error correction and compression in modem' and 'Wait for dial tone before dialing' are both unchecked. We'd recommend ticking the boxes for 'Show Bluetooth status in menu bar' and 'Show modem status in menu bar', as they'll save a bit of time in future. Click on Apply Now when you're finished.

17

If you look at the top right of your screen, the menu bar should contain a little picture of a phone. This is your modem icon and if you click on it and then click on Connect you can now test your Bluetooth connection. Make sure any other internet connections – wired or wireless – are disabled when you do this. Once you've clicked connect, click on the icon again and then select Open Internet Connect.

18

Internet Connect gives us a clear picture of what's happening, so the Status line at the bottom will change from Connecting to Authenticating User and finally, Connected To. You don't need to use this normally – just click on the modem icon and then choose Connect or Disconnect – but when you first try your Bluetooth connection it's a good idea to use it so that if there's a problem, you can see when it occurred. If you can't get a connection at all it means either your phone hasn't got a signal or it isn't set up correctly; if you can connect but get kicked out during the authentication stage, it means your account details are incorrect.

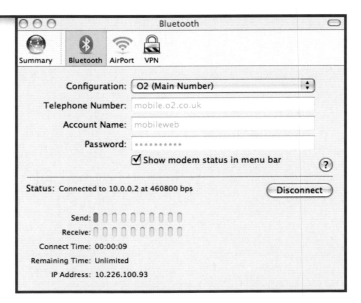

And here's the result: a real web page over a real mobile phone connection. If you look to the right of the modem icon you'll see a time display: this tells you how long you've been connected in hours, minutes and seconds. That information doesn't really matter with GPRS or 3G connections, because you're billed according to how much data you download rather than the time you take to do it, but it's crucial if you're connecting by way of a slow, pay-per-minute GSM connection.

Can I use my mobile phone if I don't have Bluetooth?

Yes you can, although if your phone has Bluetooth and your laptop doesn't it might be worth investing in a USB Bluetooth adapter. If that doesn't appeal, there are a few ways to connect through your mobile phone, depending on the type and age of phone you have. If your mobile phone can connect to your laptop with a USB cable, you can usually use it as a modem; the process is almost identical to using a Bluetooth connection, although of course you're connecting by way of a cable rather than wirelessly. The software that came with your mobile phone should take care of the necessary configuration.

With older phones and laptops, you can create a wireless connection over infra red (IRDA). Many laptops and most mobile phones have infra-red ports and the process is similar to creating a Bluetooth connection. The big difference is that infra red needs a line-of-sight connection; in practice, we've found that means putting the mobile phone's infra-red port right next to the laptop's one and hoping nothing moves them and breaks the connection.

Networking with other PCs

The simplest way to network two PCs is to run a cable or a wireless connection between them. If they're both running Windows Vista you can do all kinds of interesting things including sharing files and even sharing software. Before you can do that, though, you need to get them to talk to each other. As we'll discover, that couldn't be easier.

Sharing files on a Windows Vista laptop

We've got two Windows Vista PCs, both with networking hardware: a desktop connected by Ethernet cable to a wireless router and a laptop accessing the same router by way of Wi-Fi. Before we can get our two PCs to talk to one another we need to ensure that they're both set to discover new networks; to do this, click Start > Control Panel > Network and Internet > Network and Sharing Center and turn on Network Discovery (if it isn't on already). If this option isn't enabled, your Vista PCs won't be able to see one another.

As you can see, the Network and Sharing Center isn't much use if you're not connected to a network – and in this screenshot, our laptop's wireless card isn't switched on. The solution is simple enough: switch on the card, wait for a few seconds and let Windows Vista find and connect to our wireless network.

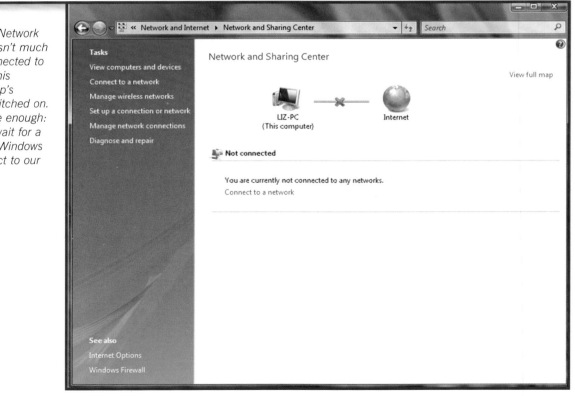

Ta-da! We're connected to the network and the icons at the top show where we fit in the great scheme of things; from left to right, there's our laptop, the router and the internet. The important bits are in the Sharing and Discovery section, though. If Network Discovery and File Sharing aren't already green, click on them to enable those features.

Click on the arrow next to Public Folder Sharing and you'll see three options: turn on sharing so anyone can access and open files; turn on sharing so people can also change and create files; and turn off sharing. We'll go for option two, which means that other computers on our network can read, write, change and delete files.

Now let's turn on our other Vista PC and see what we can do with our network. The screenshots for the rest of this walkthrough are from our desktop computer, which we'll use to connect, browse and synchronise files with our laptop.

If you click on View Full Map you should see something like this: as well as the internet connection, our desktop PC (in this screenshot, it's called Dell) can see our laptop (Liz_laptop). Right-click on the other person's computer and click Open.

As you can see, we're now looking at our laptop – or at least, the bits we've given our desktop PC permission to look at. In this example, the desktop PC is allowed to browse the Public and Printers folders.

Double-click on Public to see its contents. If you've got read-only access to this folder you'll be able to open and copy files from the other PC and if you've got full access you can rename, edit or delete the files or copy files into the folder from your hard disk by dragging and dropping.

If you wish, you can ensure that these files are always available to you even when you're not connected to the other computer. To do this, go back one step, right-click on Public and click 'Always available offline'. The Sync Center launches and makes copies on your computer of the laptop files to which you'd like permanent access. Depending on the size of the folder you've selected, this could take a while.

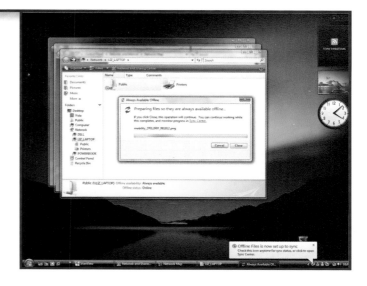

Open Sync Center from Control Panel > Network and Internet > Sync Center. You'll see that there's an entry already in there: Offline Files. Double-click on the icon to see more.

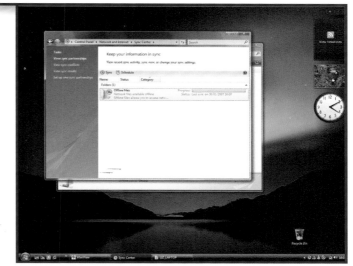

You should now see the folder you wanted available at all times, in this case the Public folder on the laptop. Click on browse to see the contents of that folder.

10

In this screenshot, our laptop is no longer connected to our network, but the files you selected are still available. The changes you make can't happen on the laptop – it isn't connected – but they are made to your local copy of the laptop's files and those changes are carried across to the originals on the laptop when you get Sync Center to synchronise your files.

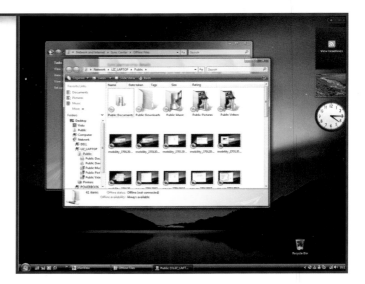

11

Close the window and return to Sync Center. Immediately above Offline Files you'll see two buttons: Sync, which synchronises files between the two PCs immediately (if the appropriate computer is connected) and Schedule, which enables you to sync files automatically at specified times or when specific things happen, for example whenever you log on to your local network or leave your PC idle for a specified time. In most cases, synchronisation happens without any problems, but occasionally you'll encounter a conflict – for example, when you've been working on a file and the other person has also been working on their copy of it. In such cases, called Sync Conflicts, Sync Center will ask which version to keep.

12

As we've already seen, you can use the Control Panel's Network and Sharing Center to limit network access – so you might want other computers to read files, but not change them, or you might restrict access to specific user names. And of course, you can turn off sharing altogether.

The trick with networking is to take a less-is-more approach and limit access to the bare minimum – so if people only need to view the files in your Public folder but don't need the ability to edit them, it makes sense to limit their access accordingly and you should use the Network and Sharing Center to give read-only access rather than full access. Conversely, you're not limited to sharing the Public folder unless you want to be. If file sharing is switched on in the Network and Sharing Center you can share any folder by right-clicking on it in Windows Explorer and clicking Share.

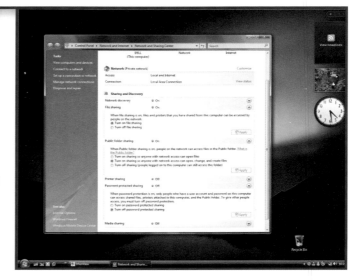

Browsing files on a Vista machine from a Mac Laptop

Although Macs and PCs have entirely different operating systems, that doesn't mean they can't talk to one another. In this walkthrough, we use an Apple Mac laptop to access the shared Public folder of our Vista laptop.

①

To connect from an Apple machine, we need to know the Vista PC's IP address – its unique address on the network. You can find this from the Networking and Sharing Center in Vista by clicking on the View Status link next to the name of your network connection. You should see the dialog box shown here. Click on Details to continue.

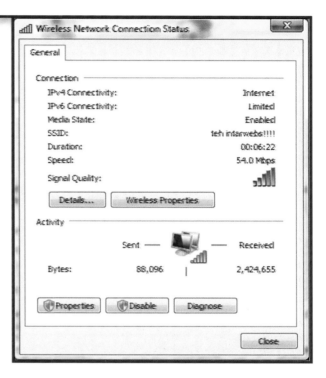

②

The number we want is labelled IPv4 IP Address and in this case the address is 192.168.0.5. Take a note of this number, click on Close and turn to your Mac laptop.

3

Click on the Mac desktop to make sure that the Finder menu
bar is on top – it should display Finder immediately to the right
of the Apple logo – and then move your mouse to that menu
bar. Click on Go and then select the Connect To Server option.

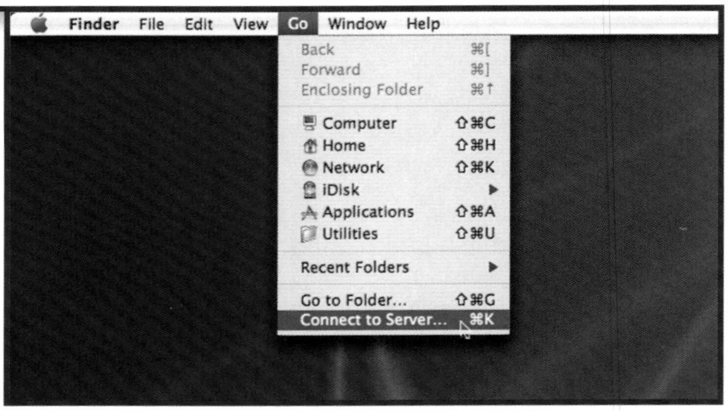

4

Remember the IP address we took a note of in Step 2? We need
it now. The easiest way to connect your Mac to a Windows
machine is to use a technology called SMB, or 'Samba'. It works
in much the same way as an internet address but instead of the
prefix http:// it uses smb:// – so to connect to our Vista PC, we
need to type smb://192.168.0.5 in the Server Address box.
Click on Connect when you've done this.

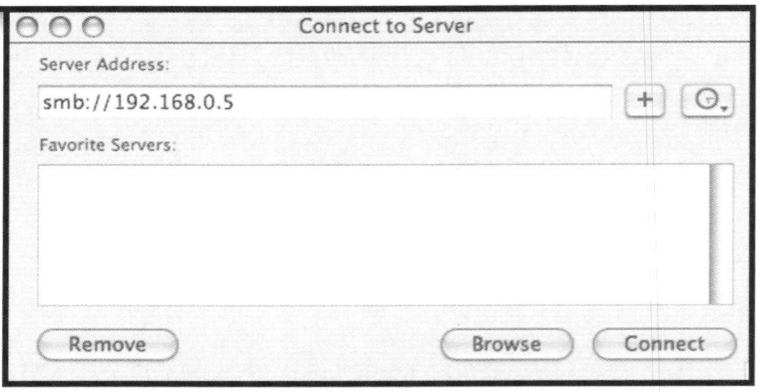

5

Your Mac will now look on the network for a computer whose
address is 192.168.0.5 – this usually takes a few seconds, so
don't worry if nothing seems to be happening. Provided you've
entered the correct IP address, your Mac will find it eventually.

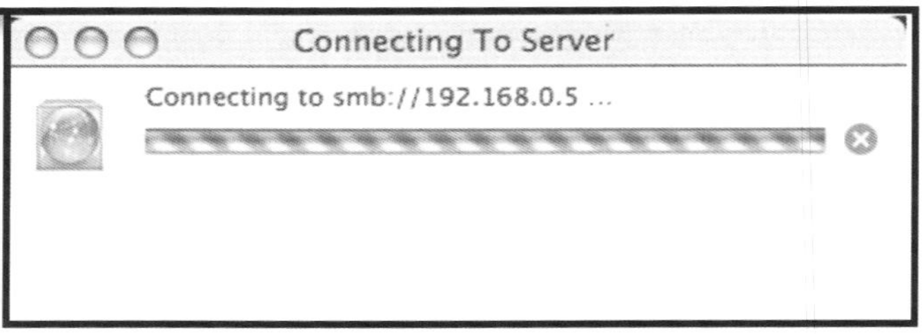

6

After a few seconds you'll see the login dialog box shown here.
The first two fields are filled out automatically (Workgroup is the
default name for Windows networks and Gary is our user name
on the Mac). If the folder you're trying to connect to is password
protected, enter the password here and then click Remember
This Password In My Keychain if you want your computer to
remember it for future use. We haven't password protected our
Vista PC, though, so just click OK here.

7

You'll now be asked which shared folder you want to connect to. In this example there's only one choice – Public – but if you've shared multiple folders you can choose the appropriate one from the drop-down menu. Click on OK to continue.

8

After a few seconds, a new icon should appear on your desktop, labelled Public. This is a shortcut to the Public folder on your Vista PC and you'll notice that the icon isn't a folder or a hard disk. That's so you can immediately see that it's a remote folder that isn't actually on your computer.

9

Your Mac will automatically open the Public folder in a standard Finder window, just as it does with normal folders. As you can see, files and folders look just as they do on your Mac – but the contents of this window are on the Vista PC, which is sitting in another room and is connected over our wireless network.

10

You can now interact with the files in the Vista PC's public folder as if they were files on your Mac. For example, you can drag a zip file from the Public folder to the Mac desktop. If the PC owner has given you read, write and change access in their Network and Sharing Center, you'll be able to drag or save files into the Public folder too. To disconnect, simply click on the eject icon next to Public in the sidebar on the left of the dialog box.

4

PART **4**

Keeping your laptop running smoothly

PART 4 Routine maintenance and preventive maintenance

Modern laptops do most of their own maintenance. For example Windows and OS X automatically connect to the internet to download program updates. That doesn't mean you're completely off the hook, though. These are our top tips for happy computing.

Every day

Many of the programs you use connect to the internet every day to see if updates are available. In the case of anti-virus software, that's a feature you shouldn't disable: new viruses appear every day and it's important to have the most up to date anti-virus files. Windows Update (on PCs) and Software Update (on Macs) will automatically check for system software updates and when you run other programs – your web browser, your photo program or your word processor – they may also check to see if updates are available.

It's worth noting that if you put your laptop to sleep at night rather than shutting it down, some daily updates won't happen. On Macs, Software Update checks for new downloads when OS X loads, so if you go days without shutting down your computer Software Update will go days without checking for patches and program updates.

Every week

Although Windows Update automatically downloads critical system files (provided you haven't turned this feature off, of course), it's still worth a weekly visit to see if there are any new updates that Microsoft doesn't deem critical. Software updates for wireless network cards and other hardware tend to fall into this category.

Every month

Check the manufacturers' websites to see if there are driver updates for your graphics card, your sound card or any other hardware in your system. Such updates can make your system more reliable and, particularly in the case of graphics hardware, the most up-to-date drivers can improve your computer's performance too. Don't forget the laptop manufacturer's site either: some firms update their own software (such as the power management tools that come with many PC laptops) and provide updates to your laptop's firmware, the system software that runs your internal and external hardware.

Take a backup of any files you can't possibly live without. If you use your laptop for work, weekly rather than monthly backups are a good idea.

Uninstall any programs you don't need and delete any old files that are cluttering up your hard disk. On Windows, pay particular attention to the startup folder: anything in here loads every time you run Windows.

If your laptop has a Nickel Cadmium battery, it's a good idea to drain the battery every few weeks. To do this, run on battery power until the battery has fully discharged and then recharge it fully before using it again. This can postpone the dreaded battery memory syndrome, which can dramatically reduce your battery's useful lifespan.

Both Windows PCs (using Windows Update) and Apple Macs (using Software Update) automatically check for important system updates. Don't switch these features off!

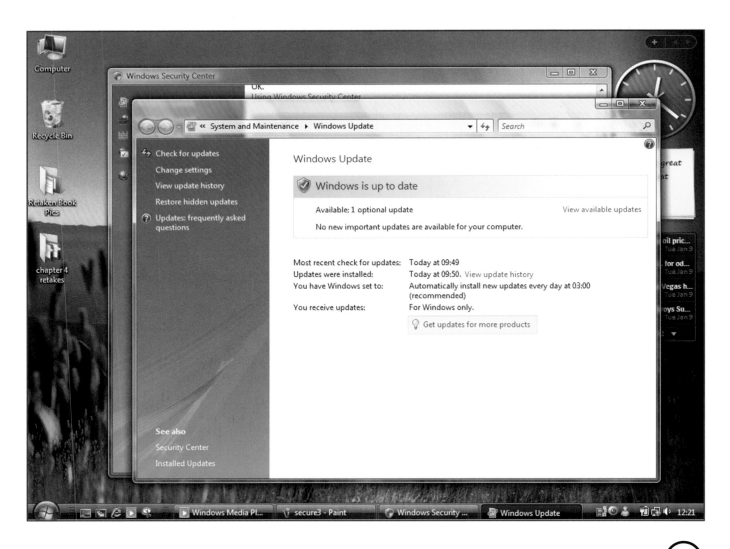

Essential security settings and software

Connecting to the internet without a full complement of security software is like jumping naked into a tank of piranha fish: sooner or later, something's going to bite you. On PCs, that's likely to happen very quickly indeed and a number of researchers have discovered that an unprotected Windows XP machine can be infected within two minutes of its first internet connection.

Security: Macs and Windows

At the time of writing, there are no viruses or other dodgy internet files that Apple users need to worry about. Almost all the world's various net nasties are aimed at Windows computers, partly because of issues with Windows XP (and earlier versions of Windows) and mainly because Windows machines outnumber Macs by a huge margin. That means Windows offers cybercriminals a much more tempting target, although as Macs gain in popularity they could well become targets too. For now, though, we think Mac OS X's built-in security tools are perfectly adequate and don't require additional security software – unless you're using Boot Camp to run Windows on your Mac, in which case keep reading.

Windows Vista is much more secure than Windows XP, which in turn was more secure than Windows 95, but no matter which version of Windows you're running we wouldn't recommend connecting to the internet or any other network without first installing security software. Some of the tools you need are built into Windows, but other important ones aren't. So what security systems should every self-respecting Windows user have on their system?

Lots of security firms offer anti-virus packages for Mac users, but at the time of writing there aren't any dangerous viruses that could affect a Mac – unless you're using Boot Camp to run Windows on your Mac.

Sophos Anti-Virus

- Macintosh HD
- PUBLIC

Macintosh HD:Applications:A ...:Contents:Resources:ABFR.icns

Items scanned: 298   Viruses detected: 0   Errors: 0

▶ Details

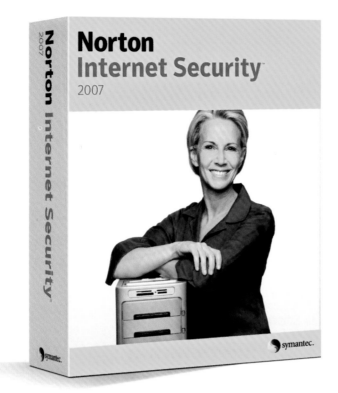

Anti-virus software

Viruses can hijack your email account, trash files or make your PC shut down for no reason and they're the most common and most annoying infections your PC can contract. Anti-virus software can detect and kill viruses on your system and it can scan incoming emails and files to stop viruses getting on to your system in the first place.

Anti-virus software needn't be expensive – you can get free PC anti-virus software from **www.grisoft.com** and firms such as McAfee, Symantec and Zone Labs all offer reasonably priced anti-virus packages – but when you're choosing a program make sure that its list of viruses is updated at least daily and that such updates are included in the price. With new viruses discovered daily, virus protection that doesn't get updated is useless – so when you've got the software, make sure you keep it up to date.

Packages such as Norton Internet Security offer anti-virus, anti-spyware and firewall protection in a single package.

Anti-spyware software

Spyware is malicious software that sneaks onto your computer and does something unpleasant. It might hijack your web browser and direct you to dodgy sites; it might send your personal data to an internet villain; or it might just blast you with ads. It's annoying, has a catastrophic effect on your PC's performance and it's a very good idea to get rid of it. Windows Vista includes a free anti-spyware program (Windows Defender) and you can download a version for Windows XP from Microsoft.com, or you could try a free alternative such as Ad-Aware (**www.lavasoftusa.com/products/ad_aware_free.php**). As with anti-virus software, make sure your anti-spyware package is updated regularly.

Windows Defender is built into Vista and is a free download for Windows XP. It scans for spyware and, crucially, it's regularly updated so that it can protect you from the latest online threats.

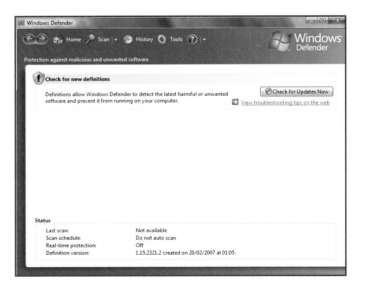

Internet Explorer 7 attempts to spot 'phishing' sites that try to con you, but in our experience it's not always successful. It pays to be suspicious – don't click on official-looking links that claim to be from your bank. They're fakes.

Reported Phishing Website: Navigation Blocked - Microsoft Internet Explorer

File   Edit   View   Favorites   Tools   Help

Phishing Filter has determined that this is a reported phishing website.

We recommend that you close this webpage and do not continue to this website.

➡ Click here to close this webpage.
➡ Continue to this website (not recommended).

❓ What is Phishing Filter?
Report that this is not a phishing website.

Anti-spam software can prevent rubbish like this from infesting your email inbox. Accuracy improves over time, but you can expect reasonably successful spam-zapping from when you first install the software.

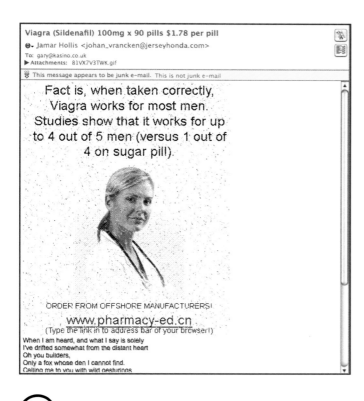

Viagra (Sildenafil) 100mg x 90 pills $1.78 per pill
Jamar Hollis <johan_vrancken@jerseyhonda.com>
To: gary@kasino.co.uk
Attachments: 81VX7V3TWK.gif
This message appears to be junk e-mail. This is not junk e-mail

Fact is, when taken correctly, Viagra works for most men. Studies show that it works for up to 4 out of 5 men (versus 1 out of 4 on sugar pill).

ORDER FROM OFFSHORE MANUFACTURERS!
www.pharmacy-ed.cn
(Type the link in to address bar of your browser!)

When I am heard, and what I say is solely
I've drifted somewhat from the distant heart
Oh you builders,
Only a fox whose den I cannot find.
Calling me to you with wild gesturings

Anti-phishing software

Internet Explorer 7 and the Firefox web browser both include features designed to spot and warn you about 'phishing', which is when scammers create believable-looking emails or websites that are designed to get your online banking details. You'll also find that many anti-spam programs include phishing protection. However, in our experience anti-phishing software can't detect every single scam, so it's important to remain suspicious. Your bank will never email you and ask for your secret login information and neither will any other finance-related site.

Anti-spam software

Spam – the slang term for unsolicited email – is a menace, with some estimates suggesting that it accounts for nearly 90% of all email traffic. Some spam is pornographic; other spam carries viruses; all spam is irritating. Anti-spam software attempts to scan incoming emails, spot the junk and get shot of it and if you use it for a period of months it becomes extremely accurate. You'll find that most security software suites include anti-spam along with anti-virus scanning.

Firewall software

Imagine you live in a huge house with hundreds of doors. You've never locked them and you've never had a problem. Then one day, thousands of burglars move in next door – and you wake up one morning to discover that they've raided your house, stolen your video and wrecked every room. A firewall prevents that from happening to your PC.

PCs were designed in a more innocent time and when they have a network connection they have lots of doors, called 'ports'. There's a port for email to come in, a port for files, another port for chat software and so on. Unfortunately in recent years, various villains have discovered ways to sneak malicious software through those ports. A firewall stops them by closing the doors you don't need and demanding identification whenever a program tries to use a port.

Firewalls do two things. They stop malicious traffic from getting into your PC and they stop programs from sneakily using your internet connection to transmit data without your permission. Both Windows XP and Windows Vista have built-in firewalls, but the one in Windows XP only blocks incoming traffic – so we'd recommend investing in a firewall that blocks outgoing traffic too.

If you have Windows Vista you don't need additional firewall software, but make sure the Windows one is actually running by checking Windows Security Center (Start > Control Panel > Security).

Windows Vista's security center includes a two-way firewall that blocks both incoming and outgoing communications initiated by malicious software. The Windows XP version only blocks incoming traffic, so it's worth investing in additional firewall software.

Windows Security Center

Windows Update
Windows Firewall
Windows Defender
Internet Options

Get the latest security and virus information online from Microsoft

Change the way Security Center alerts me

Security essentials
To help protect your computer, make sure the four security essentials below are marked On or OK.
Using Windows Security Center

Firewall — On

Automatic updating — On

Malware protection — Out of date

Virus protection — Out of date
Bitdefender Antivirus reports that it might be out of date. Bitdefender Antivirus has not provided Security Center with a program to fix this issue.
Show me my available options. [Update now]

Spyware and other malware protection — Out of date
BitDefender Antispyware reports that it might be out of date. BitDefender Antispyware has not provided Security Center with a program to fix this issue.
Show me my available options. [Update now]

Windows Defender, which is included in Windows, is also available to help protect against potentially unwanted software. [Turn on now]

How does anti-malware software help protect my computer?

Other security settings — OK

See also
Backup and Restore

How to hide your data

Anti-virus and firewall software can't do anything to prevent someone physically stealing your machine. So how can you be sure that if your laptop does fall into the wrong hands, they won't be able to get their hands on your data?

The easiest way to stop important data from falling into the wrong hands is to make sure it isn't on your laptop in the first place and you should never keep details of passwords or other login details on your computer. To protect sensitive documents, consider the use of encryption software such as Cryptainer LE (**www.cypherix.co.uk**), File Vault (free in OS X) or BitLocker (free in the Ultimate edition of Windows Vista). These programs can scramble your documents or messages using an almost unbreakable code and the only way to unscramble them again is to enter the correct password.

For really sensitive data, it's also sensible to securely wipe your hard disk if you're selling or giving away an old computer. That's because when you delete a file, it isn't actually deleted; the operating system simply removes its name from its big list of files. Eventually the operating system will stick another file on top of the old data, but until that happens it's still very easy to recover the 'deleted' file.

Secure deletion programs get rid of files permanently by overwriting them again and again with random data, making it almost impossible for anyone to resurrect your data. Most security suites include a secure deletion tool and Mac OS X's Disk Utility (Applications > Utilities > Disk Utility) offers very secure hard disk deletion as part of the operating system.

How to track your laptop

To fight car crime, many vehicles now have electronic trackers, which can locate the car in the event of theft. You can get similar technology for computers. With programs such as PC PhoneHome and Mac PhoneHome (both around £16 from **www.pcphonehome.com**), you can track down your computer if somebody steals it.

The idea behind PC PhoneHome is simple enough. Whenever you connect to the internet, it sends an invisible email message to the email address of your choice. This message contains the location of the computer. If your machine has been stolen the people behind PC PhoneHome can liaise with the police to recover your computer.

Some products go even further. Undercover (around £16 from **www.orbicule.com/products/**) doesn't just tell the manufacturers where the stolen Mac is; if it has an iSight camera, it also sends photographs of the thief. Undercover also has a plan B: if it isn't connected to the internet, it simulates a major hardware failure in an attempt to encourage the thief – or oblivious new owner – to take the machine in for repair, at which point Undercover does the electronic equivalent of shouting 'Help! I've been nicked!' to raise the alarm.

Do you need tracking software? Probably not – but when you consider that most tracking software costs less than £20, if it successfully recovers a stolen computer then you may feel that £20 is money well spent.

Tracking software such as PCPhoneHome can help you locate a computer in the event of loss or theft.

PART 4 Ten ways to improve your laptop's performance

If your laptop seems a bit slow, you can always upgrade it – and we'll show you how to do that in Part 5. However, before you reach for your credit card there's a lot you can do to make your machine run more smoothly without changing a single component and in many cases the difference can be dramatic.

Close unnecessary applications and opened windows

The more your computer is trying to do, the more slowly it will run. A web browser with lots of open windows, a music player you're not listening to, an email program checking for new messages, widgets or gadgets sitting on your desktop to provide the weather forecast… each of these programs is using valuable memory and dragging down the performance of the program you are using. If you want an immediate speed boost when you're doing something demanding, close any applications you don't actually need and close any open documents or files that you're not using.

Spring-clean the Startup folder

Some programs have an annoying habit of starting every time you switch on your computer, whether you need them or not. That means your laptop takes longer to load and it means that before you start doing anything your system's already loaded up with unnecessary programs. On a Windows machine you'll find the culprits lurking in your Startup folder. Click on Start > All Programs > Startup and see if there's anything there that shouldn't be. If there is, you can remove it in two ways. First, run the program, check its Preferences or Options menu and see if there's a 'run at startup', 'Run every time Windows loads' or similar option; if there is, disable it. If no such option is available, click on Start > All Programs > Startup, right-click on the program you want to remove and select Delete.

On an Apple machine you might encounter the same issues, but the solution is slightly different. Click on the Apple logo at the top left of the screen, choose System Preferences and then click on Accounts. Toward the top of the window you should now see a tab marked Login Items; click on this and you'll see a list of the programs that run every time you start your Mac. To stop a program from running every time, click on it and then use the minus button (immediately below the list) to remove it. Please note that simply unchecking the box next to a program doesn't stop it running; it makes the program run in the background – so while you won't see it, it's still using valuable system resources.

Stop System Restore

Windows XP, some versions of Windows Vista and Mac OS 10.5 all include 'time travel' programs that take regular snapshots of your hard disk to help you recover in the event of disaster and these programs take up lots of hard disk space and can make a slight difference to your computer's performance. To disable this feature in Windows Vista, click on Start > Control Panel > System and Maintenance > System Protection and then uncheck the drives you don't want System Restore to monitor. Now, click on Turn System Restore Off.

On the Mac, you can disable Time Machine – Apple's equivalent of System Restore – in the System Preferences screen.

Eliminate eye candy

Windows PCs use lots of special effects to make things look more exciting, but these things can make the difference between decent and desperate performance. To disable unnecessary effects on a Windows XP machine click on Start > Control Panel > System > Advanced > Performance Settings > Visual Effects and uncheck animation effects and any other visual effects you don't need. On Windows Vista you can do the same thing by clicking on Start and then right-clicking My Computer. Select Properties, Advanced System Settings > Performance > Settings.

Trash temporary files

Your laptop creates temporary files when you do almost anything. For example, when you're browsing the internet your browser keeps temporary copies of the pages you've visited, when you're writing a letter your word processor keeps a temporary copy of the document so you can undo changes and so on. Such files should be deleted automatically, but they aren't always – and a too-full hard disk can easily become a drag on your system's performance. To clear temporary files in Windows click on Start > All Programs > Accessories > System Tools > Disk Cleanup and the wizard will find and remove any temporary files you no longer need.

As ever things are slightly different on the Mac. To remove the Safari web browser's temporary files, launch the program and then click on Safari in the menu bar. You can now use one of two options: Empty Cache, which gets rid of temporary copies of visited pages, or Reset Safari, which you can use to carry out a deep clean by clearing the download history, Google searches and temporary internet files.

Poke the power settings

When your laptop is running on battery power, its power management system will slightly reduce its performance to improve battery life, but if you don't like the results you can change the power settings for maximum performance in Control Panel (PCs) or System Preferences (Macs).

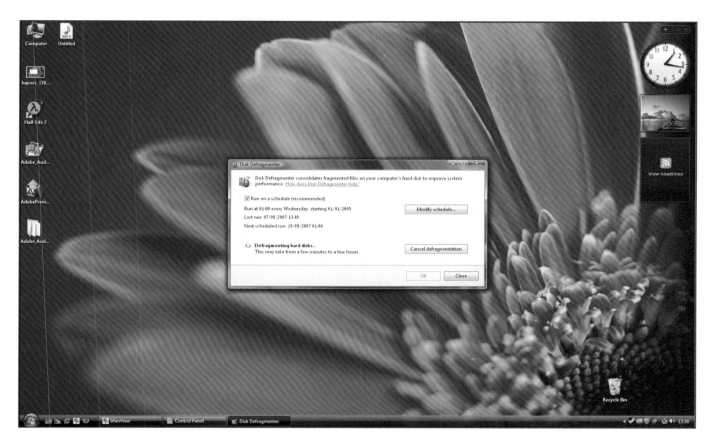

Defragment the hard disk

When a Windows computer saves a file, it often breaks it into chunks to fit the available space. Over time, that means files can be broken up and spread across the entire hard disk and the more broken up they are the more work your hard disk has to do when those files are needed. This breakup is known as fragmentation and fixing it is called defragmenting, or defragging for short. When you defrag a disk it reassembles files so that their individual pieces are as close to one another as possible and, on older laptops in particular, it can help improve performance. You'll find Disk Defragmenter by clicking Start > All Programs > Accessories > System Tools and then clicking Disk Defragmenter.

Scan for spyware

On a Windows PC, infections by spyware – malicious software that sneaks onto your PC – can cripple even the fastest computer. Most dedicated security software includes anti-spyware protection but if you don't have the tools to scan for and destroy unwanted software we'd recommend the free Ad-Aware (**www.lavasoftusa.com/products/ad_aware_free.php**), which does an excellent job of finding and killing unwanted applications.

Reduce resolution

If your system is really struggling with even basic tasks, reducing the screen resolution or number of colours reduces the load on your graphics card and can deliver a dramatic performance boost – although of course it means you'll have less on-screen room to manoeuvre. On a Mac you can adjust the display settings in System Preferences > Displays. On Windows XP, click on Start > Control Panel > Display. On Windows Vista, click Start > Control Panel > Appearance and Personalization > Personalization > Display Settings.

Abandon Aero

Windows Vista's shiny, semi-transparent Aero Glass display looks great but it's a real resource hog if your graphics card isn't particularly powerful. To disable transparency, go to Start > Control Panel > Appearance and Personalization > Personalization and then click on Change The Colour Scheme. Select the Windows Vista Basic colour scheme and then click on OK.

Troubleshooting common software faults

You'll find that, in most cases, problems with your laptop are caused by software, even though they might appear to be hardware problems. For example, if your system won't play sounds, it's much more likely that there's a problem with your sound card driver than with your sound card itself. So what kinds of faults can you expect and what can you do to fix them? Let's find out.

I'm stuck with a really low-resolution display

Windows needs little programs called device drivers to successfully communicate with your hardware and while it comes with drivers for the most common equipment it will occasionally find a bit of hardware it doesn't know about. That's particularly common with video software and, if you don't have the right driver, Windows won't be able to use your monitor properly – so instead of a 1280 x 960, full-colour display you get a jaggy 800 x 600 one. The solution? Download the most up-to-date drivers from your graphics card manufacturer and follow the instructions that come with them.

Windows Vista doesn't show the snazzy Aero Glass interface

There are three possible reasons for this. The first – and simplest – explanation is that the version of Windows Vista you have is Home Basic, which doesn't have the semi-transparent Aero Glass interface. The second possible explanation is that you don't have sufficient graphics horsepower to run it. If your video card doesn't have at least 128MB of graphics memory, Windows Vista won't let you run Aero Glass at all. The third – and, in our experience, most common – reason is our good friend the video card device driver again. If your version of Vista includes Aero Glass and your hardware has the horsepower to show it, a buggy or out-of-date video card driver is usually to blame.

My computer keeps crashing

If the crash always happens at the same time – for example whenever you try to do a particular thing in a particular program – then it's usually because of a bug in that program, so it's a good idea to check the manufacturer's site for any bug fixes, patches or program updates. If, on the other hand, the crashes seem to occur for no rhyme or reason, it could be a bug in Windows, with a device driver or with something else entirely. If you've installed new hardware or software recently and your machine was crash-free beforehand then the device drivers for the hardware or the new software are likely culprits and again you should look online for updates. Failing that, run Windows

Update to download the latest patches, bug fixes and software updates for Windows itself.

I'm getting an error message that says...

Thanks to the internet, it's now possible to check manufacturers' databases online to find out exactly what an error message means and what you can do about it. For example, if Microsoft Encarta displays an error message starting 'Enc2000 caused...' simply enter the error message into Microsoft's support site (**http://support.microsoft.com**) and you'll see a list of possible causes and solutions.

My laptop's getting very slow

This is usually a software problem rather than a hardware one and it tends to be the result of lots and lots of programs running simultaneously. Uninstall programs you don't need, run a virus scan and use a program such as Ad-Aware (**www.lavasoftusa.com**) to check for and get rid of unwanted nasties such as adware and spyware.

If the problem only occurs when you're running on battery power, that usually means your laptop's power-saving settings have been set for maximum battery life rather than maximum performance. You can change these settings in the Control Panel (on Windows) or System Preferences (on the Mac) but remember that there's a trade-off between power and battery life, so better performance means shorter battery life.

Some anti-virus programs can have a noticeable effect on your computer's performance and that's often because by default every single feature is switched on – even the ones you don't need. Go into the anti-virus software's options menu and disable anything you don't need, such as protection against viruses sent by chat software (unless of course you need that protection).

Advertising keeps appearing on my screen, even when I'm not browsing the internet

Your computer has become infected with adware or spyware. A program such as Ad-Aware will put things right.

My web browser's home page has been changed to something dodgy

Your computer has become infected with adware or spyware. A program such as Ad-Aware will put things right.

Whenever I try to burn a CD or DVD, the burn process fails halfway through

Although CD and DVD burning technology has come on in leaps and bounds in recent years, you may still find that you end up with shiny beermats instead of finished discs. Typically the problem occurs when you're doing other things at the same time as burning a disc and you'll find that closing everything but your burning software often solves the problem. If that doesn't work, the problem could be the discs themselves: we've found that the very cheapest blank CDs and DVDs can be unreliable.

PART 4 Troubleshooting common hardware faults

Laptops are reliable bits of kit, but like any other complicated electronic gadget they can suffer from the odd problem. Let's take a look at some common hardware problems, what causes them and what, if anything, you can do to fix them or prevent them from happening in the first place.

I've spilt coffee on my machine

This can be fatal to laptops and you need to take action immediately, because if liquid gets into the delicate electronics of your laptop they could do irreversible and expensive damage. Unplug the power cable, mop up any liquid you can see and then turn the laptop upside down so the keyboard is facing the ground. Leave it like that in a warm, dry place until all the liquid has dried and don't try to switch it on until then. If you're lucky your intervention will have saved the day, but if your laptop won't boot or does strange things when you switch it on then book it in for repair as soon as possible. Laptop repairers can bring a liquid-soaked laptop back from the dead, but the chance of success diminishes dramatically the longer you leave it. Don't wait for weeks, because if you do then any damage may be irreparable.

My screen's gone dark and stays that way

This usually means that the backlight on your laptop screen has failed. However, connect the power cable and check your energy saving settings first, because many laptops automatically dim the screen when running on battery power. If there's no obvious reason for the screen being dim, try connecting an external monitor: if it works fine, the problem is almost certainly a little bit of circuitry called an inverter, which controls the backlight – the bit that actually lights up your laptop's screen. Replacing it is a job for a specialist but get a quote first, especially for older laptops: the cost of the part and labour might mean that repairing the screen doesn't make economic sense.

There's a disc stuck in the drive and I can't eject it

With PC laptops, you'll usually find that there's a tiny hole in the CD drive just next to the Eject button. If you straighten a paperclip and press it into the hole, the CD/DVD drive should pop out and you can retrieve the disc.

With slot-loading drives such as the ones in Apple computers, there's no external eject switch and that means there's no little hole for you to put a paperclip into. On a Mac, you need to restart your system while holding down the trackpad button (on a Mac laptop) and this should eject the disc. If not, things get a bit more complicated. Some people recommend using a piece of thin plastic – such as a credit card – to pop the disc upwards and fish it out, but doing so runs the risk of damaging the drive altogether and we'd advise against it.

With Apple computers there are a few other steps you can try before taking the computer to a repairer and you'll find full details at **http://docs.info.apple.com/article.html?artnum=88275**. However, in many cases the only way to get a stuck disc out of a slot-loading drive is to take the computer apart, disassemble the optical drive and put it back together again. That's an extremely time-consuming and fiddly job and once again we'd recommend getting a repairer to do it.

My laptop's shutting down for no reason

Random shutdowns – when your laptop switches itself off without warning – are among the most annoying laptop faults and they can be caused by all kinds of things – including viruses. However, if your anti-virus software says that your system is free from nasties then it's likely to be a hardware problem.

The first thing to check is that the power's connected or your battery's charged, because laptops switch themselves off when the power's running low. If you're sure it's not a power problem, it may be a heat one: most laptops are designed to shut down if they overheat, so if you've been running your machine all day without adequate space around the air vents (or with the laptop lid closed while you use an external monitor) that could be the cause. Ambient temperature makes a difference too: we've noticed our own laptops having the occasional shutdown on extremely hot days.

If that doesn't work, see if there's a firmware update from the laptop manufacturer's website. Firmware refers to the programs that help your system communicate with its hardware and it's occasionally updated to fix problems. If a firmware update is available, download and run it (making sure you take a backup first) to see if that fixes the issue.

Once you've exhausted all these issues you're left with hardware problems: a faulty motherboard, perhaps, or faulty memory. If your computer has two memory modules installed you can test the latter by removing a memory chip and seeing if that solves the problem; if it doesn't, reinstall the other one and remove the second module. If the problem persists, it's time to seek professional help.

The Bluetooth button on my laptop doesn't do anything

Did it ever do anything? If the answer is no, it's quite possible that you don't have Bluetooth in your system at all. That's because many computer firms use the same cases for an entire range of laptops, but only some of those laptops actually have Bluetooth circuits installed. Using the same case even for non-Bluetooth machines saves them a few pounds.

If you do have Bluetooth installed and it's stopped working since you upgraded to Windows Vista, device drivers are probably the culprit: head for the manufacturer's website and download the up-to-date drivers, install them and reboot your system.

My memory's disappeared!

If your laptop is working fine but the amount of installed memory seems to have fallen – so for example your system says you have

512MB installed when you know there's 1GB in there – then it's possible a memory module has packed up, but it's much more likely that something's loose. If you tend to take your laptop everywhere, it's possible that the memory modules have worked loose – especially if they haven't been inserted firmly and clipped into place. Turn to Part 5 for a step-by-step guide to opening your laptop, locating the memory slots and making sure they're correctly inserted.

My battery won't hold its charge

Older laptops suffer from a problem called battery memory, which is when your battery thinks it's fully charged but it's only partially charged. This is a problem that develops over time and it's caused by running on battery power but never letting the battery go flat. It doesn't affect modern laptops' lithium-ion batteries, but on older machines with Nickel Cadmium (NiCad) batteries it can dramatically reduce battery life in a very short space of time. You can help prevent this from happening too soon by following a simple routine: every few weeks, disconnect the power cable, use the laptop until it runs completely out of power and then recharge it fully before using it again.

No matter what kind of battery you have, though, its capacity will reduce over time – and in constant use, a battery might need replacing after two or three years. That's because internal chemical changes make the battery less able to hold a charge and the effects of those changes will be noticeable in about one year.

I'm not getting any power

This is usually the fault of a broken or cracked power cable, although occasionally the culprit is the actual power connection on your laptop. If it's the former a replacement power supply will solve the problem; if it's the latter, your laptop will need its power connector re-soldered or, if you're very, very unlucky, its entire motherboard replaced.

My laptop's on fire!

We're only joking a little bit. In 2006, major laptop firms recalled their laptop batteries as the internet filled with tales of computers bursting into flames. The fault was traced to a bad batch of Sony batteries, which could in very rare circumstances overheat and go on fire. The worldwide recalls happened because the batteries were used by a variety of manufacturers; for example, they were used in Apple laptops as well as Sony ones. It's essential that you keep an eye on your manufacturer's website because battery recalls aren't unusual. If your machine might be affected, the manufacturer will provide instructions on how to check whether you have a potentially problematic battery and, if you do, they'll replace the battery for free.

If you get your battery replaced under a recall programme, don't assume that there won't be future recalls. In 2006, Toshiba recalled thousands of batteries due to a manufacturing defect and in July 2007 they announced a second recall – which affected some of the batteries they'd already replaced.

If you discover that your laptop is subject to a battery recall, you should remove the battery immediately and use mains power until your new, safe battery arrives. The risk of something going wrong in the meantime is fairly small, but when it comes to the risk of exploding batteries it's definitely better to be safe than sorry.

PART 5 Upgrading your laptop

Laptops have to cram an awful lot of technology into a very small space, so inevitably they're not as easy or as cheap to upgrade as their desktop equivalents. In most cases you're stuck with the equipment that came with your computer, but there are two key exceptions. Upgrading memory or replacing a hard disk can improve your computer's performance and capacity and both options are worth considering if your laptop's struggling with the things you're asking it to do. In this part, we discover why you might want to upgrade, how to do it and what you should try before spending any money.

PART 5

Upgrading memory

Upgrading your laptop's memory can make a huge difference to its performance and if you find your machine runs out of puff with everyday computing then inadequate RAM is usually the culprit. The good news is that upgrading your laptop's memory is quick, easy and cheap; the bad news is that you need to do a bit of homework first.

Why you might be running out of memory

Whenever you run a program, your computer copies it from your hard disk to the system memory. That's because RAM is much faster than a hard disk. However, the more programs you run, the more RAM you need – so Windows needs some RAM, your music player needs some more, your internet browser needs more still and so on. The bigger the program and the more files it has open, the more RAM is used up.

When you run out of memory your system won't usually crash, but it will slow down. That's because your computer realises it's used up all its memory, so it starts storing things on the hard disk again. The results are obvious: your computer slows to a crawl and your hard disk audibly churns away. If that happens a lot on your laptop, it's usually a sign that you don't have enough RAM.

As a rule of thumb, when you look at a program's system requirements you should take the recommended RAM and double it – so for example a program that says it wants 256MB of memory really means 'I need that amount just to get out of bed, but if you actually want me to do anything useful then I'll need even more'.

Things to try before upgrading

Adding more memory will of course make more RAM available to your system, but there are a few things you can try before spending any money. One of the easiest improvements you can make is to reduce the amount of programs running on your computer, so for example if your Startup folder is full of music players and other things you don't need, getting rid of them can make your computer run more smoothly. To get rid of programs from your Startup folder without removing them altogether, open My Computer and click on Documents and Settings > [user name] > Start Menu > Programs > Startup. Delete the programs you don't want from this folder, restart your system and you should find that your laptop feels faster.

If you're running Windows Vista, you can also try the ReadyBoost feature. This won't help with everyday performance, but it can make a difference to the 'crawling system and churning hard disk' problem we've already mentioned. ReadyBoost uses a USB memory drive or a digital camera memory card as extra RAM, instead of the hard disk. It's not as fast as real RAM but it's much quicker than a hard disk, so you should get a slight performance improvement. It's easy to use, too: simply plug the USB drive or memory card into the computer and Windows will display a dialog box asking whether you want to use it for ReadyBoost. If you click on the Speed Up My System option, Windows formats the memory card or drive accordingly and after a reboot ReadyBoost will be active.

ReadyBoost is very clever, but before you start you need to make sure your USB drive or memory card is up to the job. You'll need a minimum of 256MB storage and a maximum of 4GB and it needs to be capable of specific speeds: 2.5MB per second for random reads and 1.75MB per second for random writes. You should be able to find these details on the memory manufacturer's website – don't buy a USB drive or memory card if the figures aren't available. Windows ReadyBoost will test your memory when you first plug it in and if it's not fast or big enough ReadyBoost will simply refuse to use it.

Microsoft recommends a ratio of one to three times the amount of memory installed in your system, so for example if you've got 512MB of installed RAM then you should consider a ReadyBoost drive of between 512MB and 1.5GB. There's little point in exceeding the recommended amount because you won't get any noticeable benefit.

ReadyBoost really makes sense when your PC's suffering from inadequate memory: we picked up a 1GB high-speed SD card for our PC laptop for £11 and sticking it into the card slot on our laptop made a difference to its performance when we were running lots of applications. It's not as effective as a proper RAM upgrade, but it's a lot cheaper and it's worth a try if you already have suitable memory cards or USB drives kicking about.

Another option to consider is scanning your system for adware, spyware and other unpleasant things that sneak onto your system. Programs such as Ad-Aware (free from **www.lavasoftusa.com/products/ad_aware_free.php**) can search your system for these nasties and get rid of them and the difference can be dramatic. We were recently asked to check out a laptop that had become slower and slower over a period of months and Ad-Aware uncovered 220 different unwanted applications. Every single one of them was running and every single one of them was using RAM. You won't be surprised to read that when we got rid of them all, the laptop's performance returned to normal.

No, I definitely need to upgrade. What do I need to know?

Before you can upgrade your system memory, you need to know two things: what's already in your system and what you can add to it.

The reason you need to know what's already inside your computer isn't just because you need to order the right memory chips, although of course that's important. You also need to know what's already installed because laptops typically only have room for two memory modules and if both slots are already full you can't simply add memory without having to get rid of one or both of the original modules. Some older laptops won't accept memory unless the chips are identical, which means you can't mix and match different sizes.

In some cases you might find that you can't upgrade your laptop at all. For example, the Dell Inspiron 1000 has a single memory slot with a 256MB chip in it and it doesn't support memory modules of bigger sizes – so you're stuck with what's in it. In other cases, you might not be able to upgrade your system by much. Sticking with Dell again, the Inspiron 1100 has two memory slots that support up to 512MB apiece, so you can't install more than 1GB of RAM in total.

The easiest way to find out what's in your system (on a Windows machine) is to use Crucial's memory scanner, which you'll find at **www.crucial.com/uk/systemscanner**. This little program inspects your PC and tells you what memory configuration you have and it will also tell you what memory you can install.

The scanner is Windows-only, but it's easy to get the same information on an Apple laptop. Click on the Apple menu in the toolbar at the top of your screen, select About This Mac and then click on the More Info button. This will open the System Profiler tool, which can tell you everything about your computer. On the left side of the screen you'll see a panel labelled Contents; in that panel you'll see the word Memory. This brings up the Memory Slot information, which tells you what kind and size of memory you have in each slot.

Choosing your upgrade

1

If you've used Crucial's scanner, you'll automatically be taken to the memory chooser pages, but if you haven't then you'll need to go via their website front page. Visit **www.crucial.com/uk** *and you'll see a big box marked Crucial Memory Advisor Tool. Choose your laptop manufacturer from the drop-down list and then click on the Go button.*

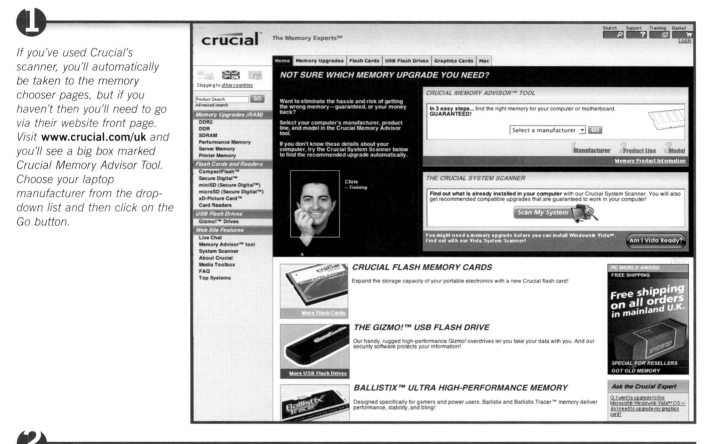

2

Depending on the manufacturer, you may now be asked to choose a product line. For example, with Dell laptops you need to choose between Inspiron and Latitude laptops, with Acer there are Aspire laptops, Ferrari-branded laptops and so on. Choose the appropriate option from the list.

Now select the specific model from the drop-down list and click Go. You'll now be taken to the upgrade page for your computer.

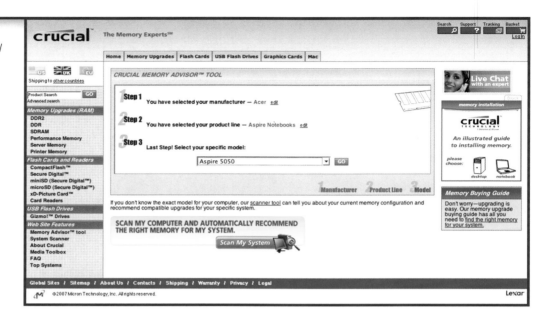

There's a wealth of information on this page. Under the heading Manufacturer Specifications you'll see details of what kind of memory your computer can accept, as well as how many slots there are. For example we've used an Acer laptop here and Crucial tells us we can install two modules of up to 2GB apiece. Pay particular attention to the memory speeds detailed here – there's no point in spending extra money on fast memory that your computer can't handle. Our Acer can handle memory of speeds of up to 5300 (the PC-5300 bit). Faster memory is available, but it won't run any faster than PC-5300 memory so it's a waste of money.

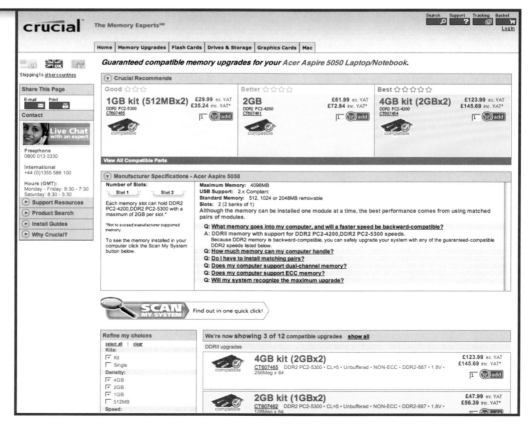

The memory advisor will also tell you whether you need to use matched memory. If the answer is yes, memory must be installed in identical pairs to get maximum performance. It will also tell you whether your system uses Error Correcting Code (ECC) memory, which is also known as parity memory. This matters because you can't mix ECC and non-ECC memory in the same system, so if your system already has an ECC memory chip and you want to keep it, you'll need to make sure the chip you buy is ECC too. This is more of an issue with older laptops; more recent ones use non-ECC memory, largely because it's cheaper.

Now, it's decision time. How much memory should you put in your system? The total amount of memory you need depends on what operating system you have and what you intend to do with it. Here's what we recommend, provided of course that your hardware can handle it:

If you're running...	and...	we'd recommend...
Windows XP or earlier	it's for everyday computing	512MB of RAM
Windows XP	your video card uses system RAM	768MB of RAM
Windows XP	it's for gaming or video editing	1GB to 2GB of RAM
Windows Vista	it's for everyday computing	1GB of RAM
Windows Vista	it's for gaming or video editing	2GB of RAM
Apple OS X	It's for everyday computing	1GB of RAM
Apple OS X	It's for graphic design or video	2GB of RAM

It's worth noting that while many laptops support up to 4GB of RAM, we can't think of any reason to install that amount of memory. For most of us, 1GB is fine and 2GB is really pushing the boat out.

You can often upgrade your memory while keeping the existing memory module that came with your computer – unless of course both memory slots have been used, in which case you can't upgrade without getting rid of one of the existing modules. Here are some examples of how you might approach your upgrade and what, if anything, you'll need to get rid of.

You've got...	You want...	Buy...	Dump...
1 x 256MB	512MB	1 x 256MB	Nothing
2 x 256MB	1GB	1 x 1GB	2 x 256MB
1 x 512MB	1GB	1 x 512MB	Nothing
1 x 512MB	2GB	2 x 1GB	1 x 512MB

One last thing to check...

A few years ago we decided to upgrade the memory in an Apple Powerbook and we followed the usual steps: we checked what was in our computer, made sure we ordered the right RAM, took every precaution when installing it and so on. When we tried to use the upgraded machine, though, we hit a problem: within minutes (and sometimes seconds) of switching it on, we'd get a major system crash. We'd never had that problem before, so the memory was clearly the culprit.

Faulty memory is rare, but it does happen from time to time – and that was clearly what we'd ended up with here. So we uninstalled it, sent it back, got a replacement and went through the upgrade process again. No joy. We got the RAM replaced again. Still no joy.

Was our laptop faulty? Not quite. After some digging around on the technical support section of **www.apple.com**, we discovered that there was a known issue with Powerbooks – or rather, one particular model of Powerbook, the 1.25GHz model with a 15 inch screen. The one we had. For no good reason that particular model was exceptionally picky about RAM and it would turn its nose up at perfectly decent chips. Once we knew about the issue we were able to speak to the memory firm about it and they found an upgrade that our laptop would actually accept.

The moral of the story? Had we checked the support forums before trying to upgrade in the first place, it would have saved us a great deal of time, worry and hassle. It's an unusual problem – provided you choose memory with the right specifications, 99% of laptops will accept it without any problems whatsoever – but it shows how a bit of homework can save you a lot of hassle.

Get the right tools and take the right precautions

Actually upgrading the memory in your laptop is easy: it's just a matter of removing a cover plate, finding the memory slots and putting the new chips in. You'll need the following tools:

- A small Phillips (X-shaped) screwdriver – it's a good idea to invest a few pounds in a set of micro-screwdrivers, because they come in handy for all kinds of computer repairs.
- A coin or a large flat-bladed screwdriver to remove the battery on an Apple laptop.
- An anti-static wrist strap or mat to ensure that static electricity doesn't get into your laptop's fragile innards. A static shock can cause serious damage to delicate components.

As with any upgrade, we'd strongly recommend backing up important files and making sure you've got the installation CDs for your software too. Things don't go wrong very often, but it's better to be safe than sorry.

There's one more step you need to take before starting work: disconnect the power. Electricity and upgrading don't mix and you should never work on computer hardware when it's connected to the mains. As laptops also have a great big batteries pumping electricity through the system, that needs to be removed too.

You've bought the right memory – so how do you install it? Although the principles of upgrading memory are the same with every computer, different firms have slightly different ways of building their machines and the memory slots aren't always in the same place. That means we'll look at two laptops: first, an Apple Powerbook; then, an Acer Aspire. As you'll see, although the specifics differ, the upgrade itself couldn't be simpler. In both cases, we recommend using an anti-static wrist strap to prevent static electricity from damaging your computer.

Upgrading RAM in an Apple Powerbook

 Disconnect the power cable and turn the laptop upside down so you can see the battery compartment and its retaining lock (the circle shown here).

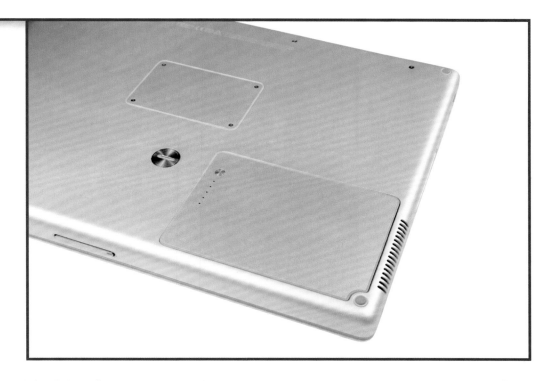

With a coin or a large flat-bladed screwdriver, turn the lock. The edge of the battery should now pop up.

Lift the battery out and put it somewhere safe. Never work on a laptop's insides when it's connected to the mains or the battery is installed.

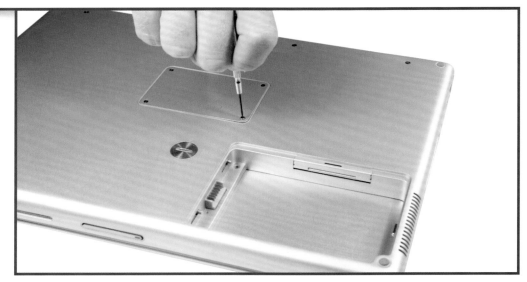

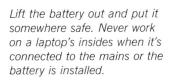

In the centre of the laptop, you'll see a small rectangular plate with four small retaining screws. This is the cover for the Powerbook's RAM slots. Remove the screws with a small Phillips screwdriver and lift off the plate. Put plate and screws somewhere safe, because you'll need them again in a moment.

You should now see the laptop's RAM slots. Our machine already has one memory module installed, but the second slot is free.

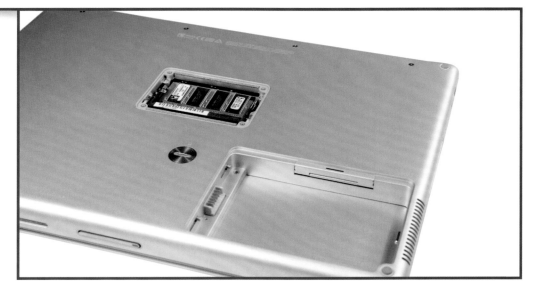

Line up the new memory module in the slot – both the module and the slot are shaped so you can only insert the module in one way. Push the module in firmly and it should slide into place.

As you push the module in, keep pushing until it sits horizontally in the slot. This should happen easily, without the need for too much force. The two retaining clips on either side of the memory slot should now click into place, holding the module secure. If the clips aren't secured the memory module may not work or might work loose.

Replace the cover plate and replace the four retaining screws. Turn the screws until they're tight and then stop – overtightening them will just strip the screw threads and damage them.

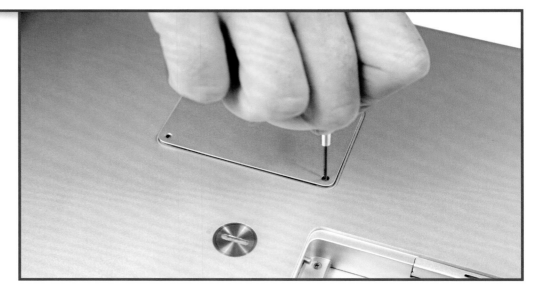

9

Slide the battery back into its compartment. The battery is shaped so that you can only insert it in the correct way.

10

Once the battery is in place, push it down until it locks in place. You can now reconnect the power cable and switch on your Mac.

11

If everything's gone according to plan OS X should now load. Click on the Apple logo at the top left of the toolbar and select About This Mac. A dialog box will now appear and next to Memory you should see the correct amount of installed memory.

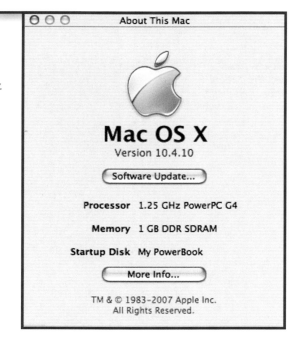

Upgrading RAM in an Acer Aspire

As with the Apple laptop, the first step is to disconnect the power cable and remove the battery. Our Acer's battery is at the back of the machine. With your fingers, slide the two retaining clips toward the left and right edges of the laptop.

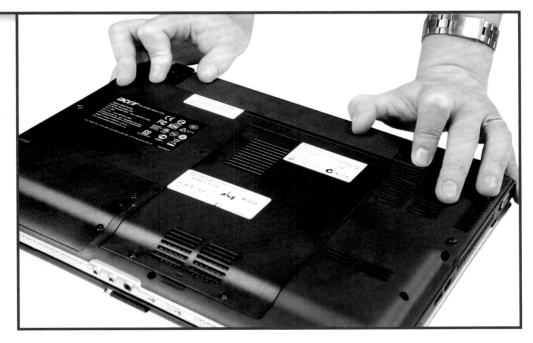

Once you've disengaged the two retaining clips the battery should slide back. If you haven't removed the battery before it might be a little stiff. Remove the battery completely and keep it somewhere handy. Never open up a laptop when the battery is still installed.

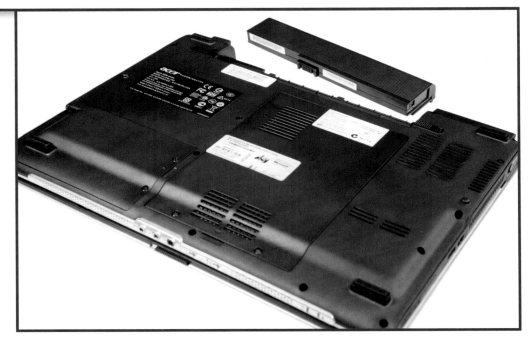

The memory slots in the Acer are located near the centre of the machine, protected by a large plastic cover. Unscrew the small retaining screws with a small Phillips screwdriver.

The protective cover is clipped in place as well as screwed in place. Using your fingers, lift the edge nearest the centre of the laptop upwards and pull it toward the front edge of the laptop. The cover should now come off. Keep the cover and screws somewhere safe.

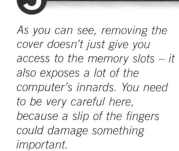

As you can see, removing the cover doesn't just give you access to the memory slots – it also exposes a lot of the computer's innards. You need to be very careful here, because a slip of the fingers could damage something important.

6

The Acer has two memory slots, one of which is already in use. Line up the new memory module in the empty slot. Once again both the memory module and the slot are shaped to prevent you from putting the module in back to front.

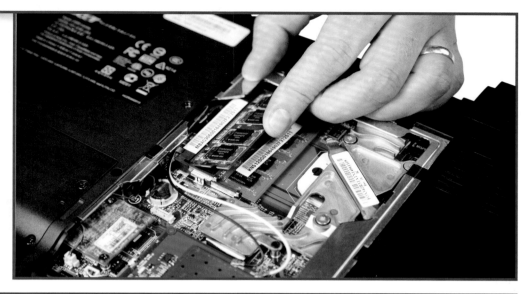

7

Push the memory module firmly into its slot. Once it's in place, push down so that the memory module is horizontal. The two retaining clips on either side of the memory slot should lock the memory module firmly in place. If they don't, the module isn't fully inserted.

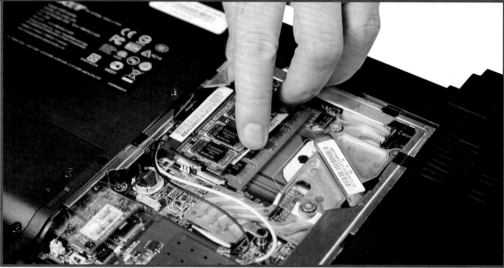

8

Retrieve the plastic cover and line it up so its tabs fit in the appropriate slots in the laptop case.

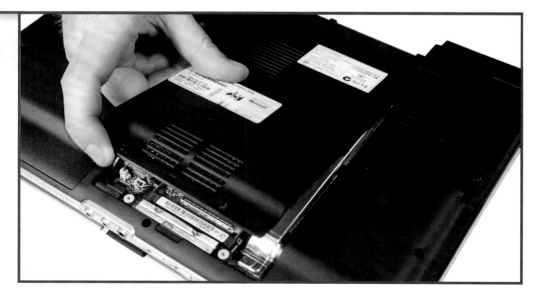

Once you've lined up the tabs, gently press down on the cover until it snaps into place. If it doesn't snap easily, check that it's lined up correctly – if it isn't and you push too hard, you could damage the cover, the case or both.

Secure the plastic cover with the retaining screws. Don't overtighten them, though: they're easily damaged.

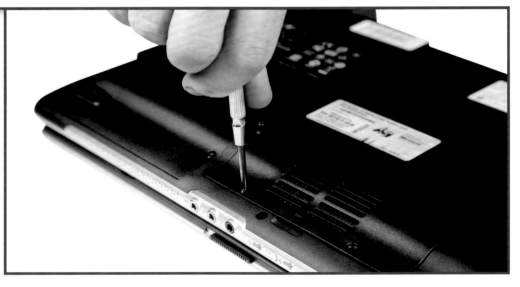

Now you can put the battery back. Line it up at the back of the laptop and gently slide it into place until the two retaining latches click shut. If the latches don't click shut and the battery is in place, use your fingers to lock the latches. It's very important that these are locked – if they aren't, your battery could fall off again.

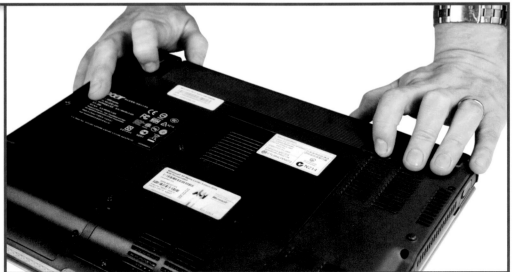

Reconnect the power and switch on your PC. When Windows loads, right-click on My Computer and select Properties. This screen tells you how much memory there is in your system and should reflect the upgraded figure. Remember that if your video card uses system RAM as video memory you'll see a slightly different figure here; for example, if you have 1GB of installed memory but the video card takes 128MB, Windows will tell you that you have 896MB of installed memory.

In this screenshot we do indeed have a video card that uses system RAM, so while we've installed extra memory to give us a total of 1GB, Windows says we've only got 766MB. The video card has grabbed the rest of our gigabyte.

Control Panel ▸ System and Maintenance ▸ System

View basic information about your computer

Windows edition

Windows Vista™ Home Premium

Copyright © 2006 Microsoft Corporation. All rights reserved.

Upgrade Windows Vista

System

Rating:	**2.2** Windows Experience Index : Unrated
Processor:	AMD Turion(tm) 64 Mobile Technology MK-36 2.00 GHz
Memory (RAM):	766 MB
System type:	32-bit Operating System

Computer name, domain, and workgroup settings

Computer name:	Liz-PC
Full computer name:	Liz-PC
Computer description:	
Workgroup:	WORKGROUP

Change settings

Windows activation

Tasks
- Device Manager
- Remote settings
- System protection
- Advanced system settings

See also
Windows Update
Security Center
Performance

Help! The upgrade hasn't worked!

Once you've installed the new memory and put your laptop back together, you should be able to start your system normally. When Windows loads, right-click on My Computer, choose Properties and the amount of memory listed in the dialog box should reflect the upgrade you've just made. On the Mac, clicking on the Apple logo and then on About This Mac will provide the same information.

Nine times out of ten, that's that: your new memory is installed, your computer sees it and everything's groovy. However, sometimes you'll find that your computer doesn't recognise the upgrade and it tells you that the amount of installed memory hasn't changed.

Provided of course that you've bought the correct memory and put it in the right place, that means one of two things. Either the new memory is faulty, or you haven't fully inserted the memory modules. The latter is the most likely explanation, so let's fix that.

Shut down the system and disconnect the power cable, remove the battery and re-open the laptop. Remove the memory modules and push them back in firmly until the retaining clips snap into place. If you have to close the clips by hand, you haven't pushed the modules in far enough. Don't feel bad – we've all done it. Once the clips are firmly in place, put everything back together and restart your system. This time, your system should correctly report the amount of installed memory.

If that hasn't fixed the problem, it's possible that the new memory modules are faulty.

Replacing or upgrading the hard disk

Laptop hard disks tend to have much less capacity than their desktop brethren, so it's hardly surprising that many laptop owners soon find that their hard disks are positively packed. Upgrading the disk drive isn't particularly difficult and we'll discover how to do it in this section – but we'll also look at some alternative options that could save you money.

Are you sure you want to do this?

Unless your hard disk has packed up, upgrades tend to happen for one of two reasons: to improve your PC's performance, or because you're rapidly running out of disk space. Upgrading your hard disk can certainly make a difference in both areas, but it's not necessarily the best option.

In both cases, a bit of housekeeping can make a big difference without costing you a penny. By reducing the amount of running programs, scanning for spyware and other unwanted software, removing programs you don't use or simply preventing unnecessary software from running every time your laptop boots, you can make a significant difference to your computer's performance. Uninstalling old programs, deleting old files and removing help files, manuals and other bits and bobs can also free up valuable disk space, so please refer to Part 4 for details on how to make your laptop happier without spending any money.

If that doesn't do the trick, there are two more options to consider. Boosting the amount of memory in your laptop will make a bigger difference to its performance than a slightly faster hard disk, especially if your laptop's running 512MB of RAM and you're using Windows Vista (or if your machine has 256MB and you're running Windows XP and so on). Upgrading from 512MB to 1GB or even 2GB will make a massive difference to your laptop's performance and we'd recommend doing that before you think about a hard disk upgrade. Turn back a few pages for an in-depth guide to upgrading memory in your laptop.

Of course, adding memory doesn't help with hard disk space, but even then an upgrade isn't necessarily the best option. Laptop hard disks are smaller (in terms of capacity) and more expensive than desktop ones and you'll find that it's often cheaper to buy a huge external hard disk and hook it up to a USB port than it is to buy an internal disk that's slightly bigger than the one you've got. For example, at the time of writing a 100GB drive for our laptop is £150 and gives us 40GB more than we have already, but we can buy a 500GB external hard disk for £88 – and unlike installing a replacement hard disk, there's no danger of damaging the insides of your laptop or invalidating your manufacturer's warranty.

If your laptop has high-speed USB ports, in most cases an external hard disk is a better bet than an upgraded internal hard

disk. The exception is when you've bought a machine whose hard disk turned out to be far too small and which is desperately short of space even after you've deleted every inessential program and file.

Know what you need

As you'd expect laptop hard disks are smaller than the equivalent desktop drives, so while a small desktop disk is a 3.5 inch drive, laptop ones are 2.5 inch. However, you can't just buy a 2.5 inch drive and expect it to work. Older laptops use standard ATA drives, but more recent ones use the newer Serial ATA (SATA) standard. SATA drives won't work with laptops that have ATA interfaces and vice-versa. The best way to find out which kind of interface your laptop uses is to check the manufacturer's website, the manual that came with your computer or the BIOS screen when your laptop boots (for example, on our Acer laptop we press F2 when the manufacturer's logo appears and this takes us into the system configuration screens that tell us what's installed in our machine).

Once you know the kind of interface you need, the next thing to look for is capacity and speed. Older drives spin at 4,200rpm but you can buy drives that spin at 5,400rpm and even 7,200rpm. Generally speaking the higher the rpm, the faster the drive – although you'll often find that there's a trade-off between speed and capacity, so the very biggest drives tend to run at slower speeds unless you're willing to spend several hundred pounds on cutting-edge kit. In most cases, that's a waste of money.

Take precautions

Your new hard disk will be completely blank, so before you think about opening up your laptop it's very important to make sure you have all the following:

- Installation CDs or DVDs for Windows (or OS X, if your laptop is an Apple one) together with any relevant certificates or registration codes
- Installation CDs or DVDs for your software programs, again with any necessary serial numbers, registration codes, unlock keys or other things you'll need to install them
- A backup of all important files, either on CD, DVD or an external hard disk drive
- Installation CDs or DVDs for additional items such as video card drivers and so on (in many cases this is your laptop's system restore disc, which will either come with your laptop or can be created from a utility on your hard disk)
- Copies of any essential information such as serial numbers for programs you've bought online, the account details for your internet connection and so on.

Another option is to make a complete drive image, which is a copy of your entire hard disk that you can then restore to a new one. On Apple computers, we'd recommend Carbon Copy Cloner, which is free from **www.bombich.com/software/ccc.html**; on PCs, we like Norton Ghost (£39.99 from **www.symantec.com**).

Windows 95 and the 32GB limit

If your laptop has been around since the days of Windows 95 and you haven't upgraded the operating system, you need to know about the 32GB limit. That's the biggest hard disk Windows 95 can deal with and if you install a hard disk with more space Windows won't be able to use it – or at least, it won't without a bit of tweaking. The solution is called Partitioning. Partitioning tricks Windows into believing that your hard disk is two disks. For example, you could install a 60GB hard disk and partition it so that Windows 95 thinks you've got one 32GB hard disk and one 28GB one.

Windows includes a utility for partitioning hard disks called FDISK, which you can copy to a floppy disk (assuming your laptop has one) to take care of the partitioning, or you could invest in third-party software such as Partition Magic which makes things less scary.

Both programs make a full backup of your files and applications and once you've fitted your new hard disk it's just a matter of installing the operating system, installing your cloning software and restoring your system. Norton Ghost can even make a bootable system disc, which means you can boot from that and restore your system without messing around with Windows discs.

There's one other thing you need to change before you perform the upgrade: if you're upgrading a Windows PC, you'll need to ensure that your system is set to boot from CD or DVD. To do this, restart your laptop and when the manufacturer's logo appears on screen, press the appropriate key to enter the system setup screen. This differs from PC to PC but the key you need should be displayed on screen at this point and it'll be something like the F2 key or the delete key.

After a moment the system Basic Input Output System (BIOS) screen will appear. Once again the specifics differ from PC to PC, but the principles are the same: you need to change the boot order, which specifies the order in which your PC should look at its drives when it's trying to find your operating system. If your hard disk is at the top of the list, your PC will look for a copy of Windows on the new hard disk and when it can't find it, it'll go in a huff and refuse to do anything else. We need to change that so it looks on the CD/DVD drive first.

Here's how to set it on a PC whose BIOS is provided by Phoenix. Once the BIOS screen appears, use the left and right arrow keys until Boot is selected and then use the up and down keys to move CD-ROM Drive so that it's higher in the list than the hard drive. When you've done that press F10 to save the changes. Now when you switch on your laptop it checks the CD drive before it looks at the hard disk – which is exactly what we need it to do so that we can install Windows.

The tools you'll need

As with any PC upgrade, we'd recommend the use of an anti-static wrist strap or mat to prevent static electricity from damaging your PC and you should always disconnect the power cable and remove the battery before opening up your laptop's case. You don't need any special tools to perform a hard disk upgrade: one small Phillips screwdriver is all you require.

Upgrading the hard disk in a Windows laptop

Once again we're upgrading our trusty Acer Aspire. Different manufacturers have slightly different approaches – so for example Acer very kindly provides a separate plastic cover for the hard disk that makes it easy to locate and upgrade, but other firms may require you to remove the entire panel from the base of the laptop – and retaining screws may be in different places, but the actual upgrade process will be identical.

Acer very kindly gives the hard disk its own protective cover and marks it with an icon of a hard disk so you know what it is. You'll find that many recent PC laptops will be similarly upgrade-friendly.

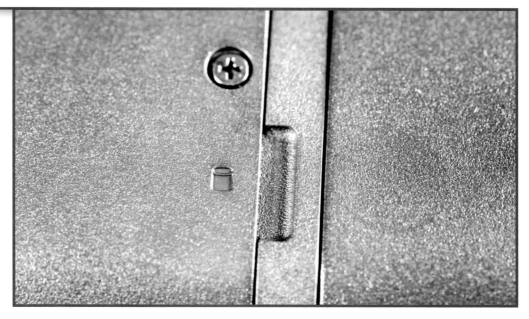

Using a small screwdriver, unscrew the retaining screws holding the plastic cover in place and keep them somewhere safe. Small screws are very hard to find if you drop them on a deep pile carpet.

Besides the retaining screws, the cover plate is held in place with plastic clips. Lift the cover firmly to disengage the clips and put it to one side.

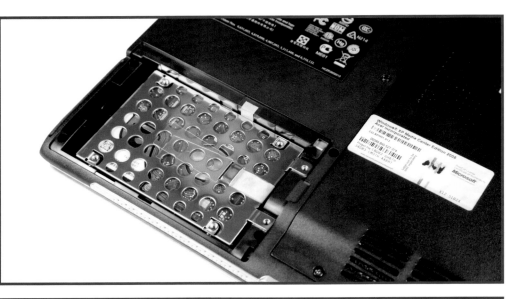

The hard disk is secured with a single screw at the edge furthest away from the centre of the laptop. Remove this screw carefully. Murphy's Law says that once you've unscrewed it, the tiny screw will now fall inside the laptop. Simply invert the laptop and give it a very gentle shake to retrieve the screw.

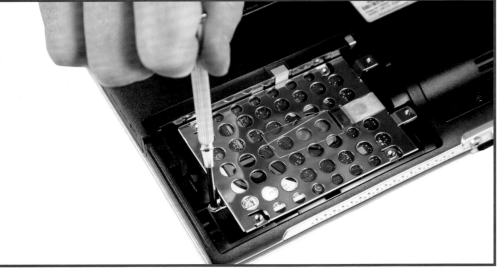

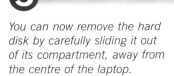

You can now remove the hard disk by carefully sliding it out of its compartment, away from the centre of the laptop.

The hard disk drive is enclosed in a protective metal cage, which is usually secured with two or four little screws. Remove the screws and the cage should simply lift off. Don't lose the screws – you'll need them again in a second.

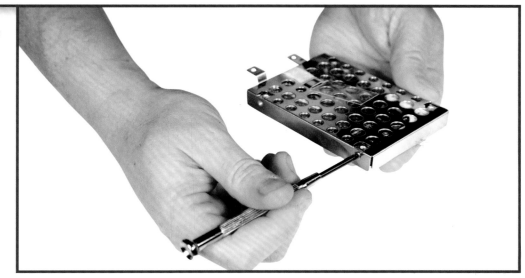

You now have an empty cage ready for your new hard disk. To fit the replacement, simply follow steps 1 to 6 in reverse: fit the cage, secure it with screws, slide the hard disk into position, secure it and replace the cover.

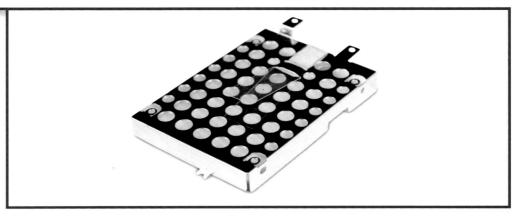

Turn on your PC and put the Windows installation disc (or your boot disc, if you used Norton Ghost to copy your old drive) into the CD or DVD drive. When the message 'press any key to boot from CD/DVD' appears, press a key and then follow the on-screen instructions. Once Windows is installed, you can then install your software and copy your files from the backups you made earlier.

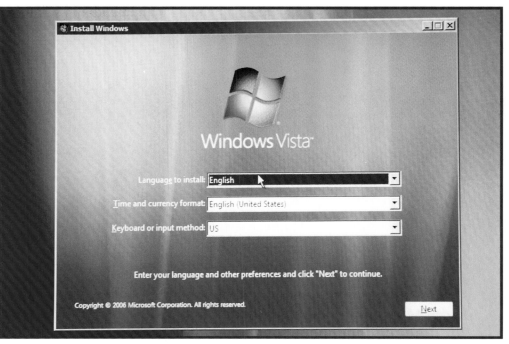

Upgrading a Windows XP laptop to Windows Vista

With very few exceptions – such as end-of-line stock sold by bargain-basement retailers – every new PC laptop on sale today runs Windows Vista, the most recent version of Microsoft's operating system. It looks nicer than Windows XP, offers much better security and it comes with the latest editions of various useful tools such as a video editor, Windows Media Player and so on. We like Windows Vista a lot, but is it worth upgrading if your laptop is happily running Windows XP? Before you decide, it's worth thinking about the following key issues.

It's hardware hungry

A laptop with a fairly old processor and 512MB of RAM is a perfectly good Windows XP machine, but it probably won't be up to the task of running Windows Vista. Vista is famously memory hungry and we think a machine with less than 1GB of system RAM will struggle – so if you plan to upgrade, you might need a memory upgrade too.

If you want to use Vista's snazzy, semi-transparent Aero Glass interface you'll need a reasonably powerful graphics card too. If your graphics card doesn't have at least 128MB of video memory and doesn't support the Microsoft 3D graphics standard DirectX 9, you won't be able to use Aero Glass at all.

Some versions aren't worth bothering with

Rather than releasing one or two versions of Vista, Microsoft has released several – and some of them aren't worth bothering with. The cheapest version of Vista, the Home Basic edition, doesn't include some key features: Aero Glass, the Mobility Center for laptop computers, Windows Media Center, a system backup utility and so on. That means it's fine if all you want is a stripped-down operating system for basic PC use, but if that's what you need then you've already got Windows XP.

Our pick of the range is the Home Premium edition, which is particularly affordable if you buy an OEM version from a site such as **Dabs.com**. OEM versions are supposed to be sold with PC hardware, so you may also need to buy a cheap mouse – but it's worth it, because the OEM version is a fraction of the price. You don't get manuals, though, and the OEM licence prohibits you from transferring Vista to another machine if you replace your laptop in the future.

There's no compelling reason to upgrade

Upgrading to Vista costs money and because it's more hardware hungry you might find its performance slower than your existing copy of Windows XP. All the reasons to upgrade are fairly minor ones – improved tools, a nicer interface, better games – and while Vista is much more secure than Windows XP, if you've invested in a decent suite of security software and kept it up to date then that's not a big issue either.

Then again...

Despite the issues we've outlined above, Vista does have some goodies to offer laptop users. Its power management system is superb and offers complete control over every aspect of your computer, enabling you to get the best possible trade-off between performance and battery life. Putting your laptop to sleep and waking it up again is faster than with Windows XP, there's excellent support for external monitors and if you plan to deliver presentations you'll like Vista's presentation settings, which make it easy to ensure your laptop doesn't go to sleep halfway through an important slide.

Do those features justify the upgrade cost (and perhaps the cost of a memory upgrade too)? That's for you to decide, but Microsoft provides a tool that can help you make that decision. The Windows Vista Upgrade Advisor is a free tool that will scan your system and warn you of any potential problems, so for example if you don't have enough RAM or your laptop contains hardware that isn't compatible with Vista, the Advisor will tell you. You can download it for free from this rather unwieldy web address: **www.microsoft.com/windows/products/windowsvista/ buyorupgrade/upgradeadvisor.mspx**

Performing the actual upgrade

You've decided to upgrade and you're clutching the install disc in your hands. So how do you actually upgrade the system? As with all upgrades, make sure you've got a backup of any important files and make sure you've got the installation discs for your various programs (or their serial numbers, if they're internet downloads). Then it's just a matter of putting the disc in your CDor DVD drive and following the on-screen instructions.

Clean or upgrade?

When you run the Vista installer you'll be given two installation options – clean or upgrade – unless you're installing an OEM copy, in which case the upgrade option isn't available. That's because OEM copies are designed to be installed on brand new PCs where there's nothing there to upgrade. In that case the choice is made for you, but with non-OEM versions you need to decide which kind of installation you'd like. As you'd expect, there are pros and cons for each method.

An upgrade installation is the simplest, because it installs Vista on top of Windows XP. That means your files, folders and programs and key settings such as your internet connection settings should be left intact, which saves a lot of hassle. However, you might find that some of the programs that worked happily on Windows XP need updating to work with Vista and because you're sticking a new version of Windows on top of the old one you might inherit any nasties that have sneaked onto your Windows XP system. You'll lose some hard disk space too: the installer moves your existing copy of Windows to a folder so you can revert to Windows XP if you change your mind later.

A clean install means you're starting from a blank slate and it's far and away our preferred installation method. It does mean that you'll need to install all your software once you've installed Windows, either from their installation CDs or by downloading them from the internet and you'll need to enter your internet account details, passwords for wireless networks and so on. However, we think the benefits outweigh the disadvantages.

Once you've installed it

Whichever installation method you choose, once the installation process is finished it's important that you run Windows Update (Start > All Programs > Windows Update) to download the latest bug fixes and security patches for Windows. At the time of writing Vista has only been on sale for a few months, but Windows Update is already packed with essential downloads to make your system more secure and more reliable.

Besides running Windows Update you should also see whether there are new drivers available for your graphics card – there probably will be – and you should update your anti-virus and security software to make sure nothing unpleasant can sneak onto your system.

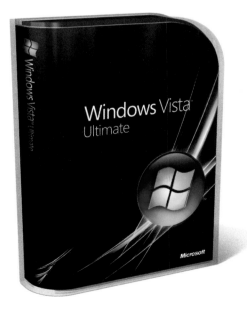

There are several different versions of Windows Vista, ranging from the Home Basic edition to the all-singing, all-dancing Ultimate edition.

PART **6** LAPTOP MANUAL
Appendices

PART 6

Appendix 1: Preventing data disasters

Murphy's Law says that anything that can go wrong will go wrong. If your entire work or life is on your laptop then losing your data can be disastrous. As we'll discover, it's easy to make sure your valuable information is safe.

Computers are generally very reliable, but there are a number of potential problems that could destroy your valuable data. Over the years, we've experienced all the following:

- Accidentally overwriting important documents with blank ones
- Accidentally deleting entire folders full of important files
- Moving files to CD to free up hard disk space – and then losing the CD
- Upgrading the operating system and choosing the 'clean install' option by mistake, erasing the entire hard disk
- Installing a software update that corrupts important data
- Spikes in the power supply causing a crash and corrupting data
- Complete and catastrophic hardware failure

You can protect against some of these problems – using a surge protector between the mains electricity and your computer can prevent power spikes, being really careful can prevent the accidental overwriting or erasing of documents and anti-virus software can prevent malicious programs from damaging your data – but not all them. And they aren't the only potential problems. Every year, data recovery firm OnTrack compiles its Top Ten Computer Disasters and in recent years the top tens have included these catastrophes:

- The man who accidentally deleted every single digital photo of his new-born baby
- The woman who tripped and dropped a heavy pot on her computer, smashing it to smithereens
- The man who attempted to fix a hard disk failure by taking his computer apart and realised halfway through that he had no idea what he was doing
- The dog that thought a USB flash drive was a tasty toy and chewed it to bits
- The man whose laptop mysteriously crashed all the time, because – as he eventually discovered – his nephew would repeatedly punch it whenever it ran slowly
- The medical company worker who spent several days processing 1,200 customer billing entries and then lost the lot when lightning struck the transformer next to the building
- The buildings expert who took his laptop with him to a construction site and watched in horror as a reinforced steel beam fell on it
- The executive who placed her laptop on the roof of her car while she opened the car door; distracted, she forgot about it

– and when she put the car in gear, the laptop fell off the roof and landed on the ground; none the wiser, the executive promptly reversed over it
- The writer who got so fed up with her computer, she attacked it with a hammer
- The company director who tried to catch up on work while having a bath and dropped his laptop in the water
- The man on a moped whose laptop fell from his bag as he went round a corner; it fell under the wheels of a lorry

Of course, few of these things are likely to happen to you (although we're sure we're not the only ones who've felt like attacking our computers with a hammer from time to time) and the reason OnTrack publishes the top tens is because in every case, the firm successfully recovered the customers' data. They'd hardly publish a list of their top ten failures, after all. However, data recovery costs money and takes time. Had the unfortunate owners made backup copies of all their important files, they could have used those backups on another computer and returned to work almost immediately – without losing a single document.

Don't assume your insurer will pay out

In July 2007, the Consumers' Association surveyed 46 UK insurance companies and discovered that not one of them would pay out if a virus or mechanical failure wiped out valuable data – so for example if you've spent months buying digital music from a shop such as iTunes and then your hard disk fails, you're not covered. iTunes won't help either, because there's no way to re-download your library without buying every single track again. 79p per song doesn't sound like much, but if you've downloaded hundreds or even thousands of tunes restocking your music library could be extremely expensive.

It's not all bad news, though. In the same survey, the Consumers' Association found that around half of insurers did cover digital downloads lost due to fire, theft or flood – but during their research they also found that some insurers' staff didn't know about such cover and some insurance documents didn't make it absolutely clear what is and isn't covered.

Here's the Consumers' Association's advice on how to keep your expensive downloads safe:

- Check your policy documents, or call your insurer directly, to see if you're covered
- Keep any receipts or bank statements relating to digital downloads you've bought
- Make sure that your systems have anti-virus software, anti-spyware and a firewall installed as hardware or mechanical failure are rarely protected
- Protect your digital content with a back up copy, particularly if you're not covered by insurance
- Consider switching insurance companies to avoid disappointment

We think that you should back up data no matter what you keep on your hard disk. If it matters to you, back it up.

The backup you absolutely, positively, 100% need to make

Many PC laptop manufacturers don't give you any system discs and that means you don't get a Windows disc – so if Windows becomes corrupt, you're snookered. To prevent this, your laptop will include a utility with a name such as System Backup Utility and this enables you to create a system recovery disc or discs on plain old CD-R discs. If you have such a utility, it's essential that you use it. If you don't and something happens to prevent you from booting your system, you'll have to pay the laptop firm for a set of system discs – which means a bill of £50 or more and a long wait for the postman.

As you can see from our table of backup methods there are a number of ways to make backups and the method you choose depends on your particular requirements. However, the principles are the same no matter what method you choose: if you need it, back it up – and back it up regularly. That means all your important documents, but also address books, spreadsheets, accounting records or any other files on which you depend.

In some cases it's also a good idea to have a paper copy of key data, so for example if you're self-employed and use an Excel spreadsheet to track your income, expenditure and tax liability then it's worth taking a printout as well as making regular backups. If you're exceptionally unlucky and disaster strikes not just your computer but your backup too, you've still got the printed copy to refer to.

How often should you make a backup?

You should always make a backup before doing anything big, such as installing a software upgrade, adding new hardware or taking your laptop on a business trip – or after anything big, such as when you complete a large project or reach the end of a quarter or financial year. In addition, you should make regular backups too.

The frequency of your backups depends on how much you use your computer and what type of backups you prefer to make. For example, if you've got an external hard disk drive there's no reason you couldn't make a new backup every day (the software that comes with the disk drive can usually do it for you: just tell it when you want it to backup your system and it takes care of the rest) – and if you spend all day every day entering data or creating things on your computer, then a daily backup would be a very good idea. On the other hand, if you spend most of your time on the phone, only use the computer for basic record keeping and back up your files to CDs, a daily backup would be unnecessary and far too time-consuming.

There's no right or wrong backup method and there's no law that says you must back up daily, weekly or monthly, but whatever method you choose and whatever frequency you decide upon, it's important to stick to a routine – so if you plan to backup weekly, make sure you do and that you keep the backups somewhere safe. You can be confident that if you skip a backup or misplace your CDs, that's when disaster will strike.

Backup methods: the good, the bad and the ugly

The method	The good	The bad	The ugly
Backing up to your own computer	It's very fast and very easy; it protects you against accidental deletion or damage to key files; if you use Windows XP or Windows Vista, the software – System Restore – is already on your computer.	Your backup is on the same computer as the original files.	Theft, hardware failure or user error could mean you'll lose the originals and the backup too.
Backing up to another computer	You don't need any additional hardware other than a network cable.	You'll need to get to grips with basic computer networking. It's not too difficult, but it's a bit time consuming.	You need to have a second computer – which is an expensive option if it's only being used for backups.
Backing up to floppy disks	Floppy disks are exceptionally cheap.	Floppy disks have tiny storage capacities; backing up even a few files is painfully slow.	Most modern PCs don't come with floppy disk drives. Disks can be wiped by magnetic fields.
Backing up to CDs or DVDs	Discs are very cheap; one CD is the equivalent of hundreds of floppies and DVDs are bigger still.	You might need extra software; for big backups on CD, you'll still need lots of blank discs.	Discs are easily scratched and there are concerns over their longevity – especially with cheaper products.
Backing up to an external hard disk	Massive storage capacities and very fast data transfer speeds mean it's the fastest way to make big backups.	If there's a disaster in your house, the external hard disk could be affected too.	Hard disks are much more expensive than a 10-pack of blank CDs.
Backing up to an internet storage site, or your own web space	Your backup is stored far, far away. It's relatively easy to do. There are lots of firms offering online backup, many of them for little or no money.	It's pointless if you don't have a broadband connection; even then, it's often painfully slow; there are potential security risks too.	If your broadband connection has usage limits, backing up could exceed them. Are you confident the internet company will stay in business?
Making printed copies of important data.	It's quick, cheap and easy and you don't need special tools to do it.	Keeping printouts isn't practical if you have huge quantities of data.	If the original files get damaged, you'll need to type it all back in again.
Not backing up at all	It requires no time, money or hardware.	You don't have a backup at all – you're tempting fate.	Disaster will strike and, when it does, you'll lose everything.

PART **6**

Appendix 2: Keeping your kit safe

Portability is a great thing, but taking your laptop out and about means it'll inevitably be exposed to more hazards than a PC that spends its days on your desk – and because your laptop is a self-contained system in a single box, damage to one bit means the whole machine is damaged. So how can you keep your kit safe?

Do you like horror stories? Here's a whole collection: according to research firm Gartner, 10% of laptops are stolen every year, a further 15% suffer serious hardware damage and the UK government lost more than 1,300 laptops, in 2001 alone, through forgetfulness (such as leaving laptops in the back of taxis) and theft. The FBI estimates that 97% of stolen computers are never recovered. In just two years, the Thames Valley Police area suffered nearly 3,000 laptop thefts. Most of those were stolen from parked cars and the *Sunday Times* reports that, in most of the UK, the detection rate for such thefts has fallen to zero.

Theft might not just deprive you of your computer. If you're lucky, your lost or stolen laptop will be wiped and re-sold – but if you're unlucky and you keep sensitive data or personal information on your computer, criminals could use it to cause you further harm, for example by accessing your online banking service and cleaning out your account.

So how do you keep your laptop safe from the light-fingered and prevent accidental damage? The good news is that there are lots of options and they're easy as well as affordable.

Laptop cases

A laptop case is an essential investment to protect your PC from knocks and shocks, but don't just rush out and buy the first one you see. That's because there are two kinds of laptop case: the ones that will hurt you and the ones that won't. If you're planning to travel with your laptop – particularly if you're planning foreign travel with lots of hanging around airports – then it's important to remember that your laptop case won't just hold your laptop. It might also hold your phone, your top, a few books, a bottle of water, your music player, some important documents, a couple of magazines you picked up at the newsagents…before long you're carrying half your bodyweight and cursing the day you chose a cheap laptop case. So what should you look for?

The most common kind of laptop case is made of nylon and looks like a briefcase. Such cases can be cheap – but not always, especially if you go for designer brands – and typically have a carrying handle and a single shoulder strap. They also have various pockets and zipped panels for holding documents, magazines and so on.

Briefcase-style laptop cases are good for business users, but it's important to check a few things. The most obvious feature is storage space, but pay close attention to the shoulder strap. If it doesn't have a movable shoulder pad that strap will soon leave nasty welts in your shoulders and the more padding it has the less painful it will be if you're lugging your laptop around for long periods. Pay attention to the make-up of the case too: the bit for your laptop should be padded to prevent the odd knock damaging your precious cargo.

Besides briefcase-style laptop bags, you can also get ones that look more like rucksacks. There are two advantages to these. First, it's not obvious that you're carrying a laptop, which can make you less paranoid about being mugged; and second, they have twin shoulder straps to spread the weight. Some models also have additional straps for your chest and your waist, which spread the weight even further and come in particularly handy when you're transporting heavier laptops, chargers and other paraphernalia. Again, make sure the straps are sufficiently padded, that the laptop's sufficiently protected and that there's enough storage space for the various bits and bobs you're bound to accumulate as you travel. Pay particular attention to the bit of the case that sits against your back: if it's not padded, it will soon start to rub against your back or let the contents of the case dig into you. Neither of these things is particularly pleasant.

If you only need to protect your laptop case as you travel from the car to an office, then a basic briefcase-style bag will be fine. However, for serious travellers we think the rucksack-style bag is a much better bet. However, what really matters here is the padding on the straps, so a well-padded briefcase-style case will be less painful than an unpadded, rucksack-style case.

Laptop locks

Firms such as Kensington (**www.kensington.com**) make a range of laptop locks, which work in much the same way as bicycle locks: they plug into the side of your computer and can't be unlocked without the unique key. The lock is on the end of a super-strong loop of steel cable that can't easily be cut and such locks are well worth considering if you're likely to be leaving your laptop unattended in an office or hotel room.

Other hazards

The same hazards that threaten a desktop PC also apply to laptops, but the damage they can do is much more serious. For example, tripping over a cable (or having a cable grabbed by a toddler or pet) can send the connected bit of kit crashing to the ground, which is bad enough if the kit is a £100 monitor but a complete catastrophe if it's your £1,000 laptop. Similarly spilling liquid on a keyboard is a problem with a desktop PC that may require you to buy a new keyboard – but if you spill your coffee on a laptop keyboard, the fragile circuits are likely to get drenched and damaged too. Be very careful with your power cables and avoid eating or drinking near your machine.

Travelling exposes your laptop to other dangers too. Never, ever put your laptop in baggage that's going into an aircraft hold – current security regulations prohibit that anyway, but even if they're lifted a quick look at how baggage handlers treat your luggage will persuade you to carry your machine as hand baggage – and if you're travelling by car, don't put your laptop bag on one of the seats. There are two reasons for that. First, it's easy for someone to open the door and grab your computer while you're sitting at traffic lights; second, emergency braking could turn your laptop into a very heavy and very expensive flying

Laptop locks, such as this one from Kensington, can frustrate even the most determined laptop thief.

projectile. If it's in the front seat, it could end up being smashed to smithereens; if it's in a back seat, you could end up with several kilograms of plastic and metal hitting you in the back of the head.

Burning batteries

In late 2006 and early 2007, some laptop owners discovered a surprising new feature: their machines exploded. The culprits were dodgy batteries and all the big-name battery firms embarked on massive recall and replacement programmes to ensure that no other machines would go on fire. Such faults are mercifully rare, but it's a very good idea to keep an eye on your laptop's manufacturer's website just in case a fault could damage your prized possession.

What you really need to know about insurance

If you leave your laptop on a car seat and it gets stolen, your insurance probably won't pay out: with most policies, valuable items such as laptops must be locked securely and out of sight in the boot or you're not covered. You'll find almost every policy demands that you take 'reasonable precautions' to 'safeguard the property'. Even if you do take precautions you might still be in for a shock: many car insurance policies have strict limits on what they'll pay for theft from your vehicle, so for example our current policy has a £200 limit – around one tenth of our laptop's actual value (some home insurance policies offer better cover, as we'll discover in a moment). Many car boots have false floors that enable you to store valuables and, if your car has such a feature, we'd recommend using that – or better still, taking your laptop with you when you park.

More and more home insurance policies automatically cover you for computing equipment, but it's important to make sure – particularly if you're using your laptop for business. For example, if you get home insurance from Direct Line you get £5,000 of cover for your home office equipment, but your work must be 'confined to routine paperwork and telephone calls or registered childminding'. If you do other kinds of work, you aren't covered.

Some firms provide special cover for laptops, which can be useful if you regularly travel away from home. Again, watch the terms and conditions: Cornhill Direct's home insurance policy does indeed cover laptops, but only if they're for personal, not business, use. If you want to cover a business laptop, you'll need to ask for and pay for, the extra Home Worker cover.

If you're buying a really expensive laptop, make sure that the insurer provides sufficient cover for each item. For example, at the time of writing the Royal Bank of Scotland provides £5,000 of cover for home office equipment, but it has a per-item limit of £1,500 for any items not specifically named in your policy documents. Similarly More Than's home insurance policy covers business equipment up to £7,500, but again its per-item limit is £1,500 – and there's a limit of £1,000 for items stolen from a motor vehicle. It's bad enough having an expensive laptop stolen,

but discovering that you're only covered for half of its value adds insult to injury.

Other exclusions are potentially more serious. In the case of More Than's home insurance, there's a very big exclusion under 'Theft or attempted theft': you're not covered 'if your home is used to receive visitors in connection with your business operating from your home'. Most insurers have similar exclusions, which is why it's so important to read the small print carefully – or you could end up with a policy that won't pay out if disaster strikes.

Remember too that your insurance might not cover the actual data on your computer. As we discussed in Appendix 1, at the time of writing, no British insurers will pay out for data loss due to viruses or hardware failures and around half of insurers won't cover expensive digital downloads – music, software, video and so on – for fire, theft or flood.

Are warranties worth it?

Computer hardware can and does fail. If a key component packs up, your entire laptop is useless. So is it worth paying for an extended warranty when you buy your machine? The answer depends on how important your laptop is to you and whether you can afford to spend time without it.

If you don't pay for an extended warranty or support package, you're still covered in the event of disaster. Most manufacturers offer a 1-year warranty and you're also covered under the Sale of Goods Act. However, standard warranties are usually return-to-base, which means the manufacturer will collect your machine and send it away for repair – and it won't provide you with a replacement to tide you over. Many firms put a strict time limit on such repairs – for example, Dell promises to fix a faulty business PC within six days – but others don't and repairs can take a while. When our laptop recently developed a minor fault, we had to manage without it for six weeks.

Computer firms will typically offer two kinds of extra cover: longer warranty periods, or enhanced services. You could replace the one-year warranty with a three-year one, or perhaps boost the level of cover from return-to-base to on-site service. Naturally this costs money. For example, to increase the cover on an Apple MacBook Pro from one year to three years, you'll pay an extra £279; if you want to upgrade the cover on a £300 Dell to include accidental damage, you'll pay an extra £70.50. That sounds reasonable, but it's a quarter of the price of the computer – and your home insurance policy may already include accidental damage cover for all your electronic equipment, not just your PC.

Different firms offer different warranties, so if you're finding it hard to choose between otherwise identical (and identically priced) machines, go for the one with the better warranty package. However, if you're considering paying extra for an extended warranty check what it covers very carefully. It's also worth shopping around: for example if you buy a laptop direct from Apple you get a 1-year warranty, but if you buy the same machine for the same price in a branch of John Lewis you get a 2-year warranty.

Index

ACKNOWLEDGEMENTS

Author	**Gary Marshall**
Copy editor	**Shena Deuchars**
Photography	**Iain McLean**
Page build	**James Robertson**
Index	**Shena Deuchars**
Project Manager	**Louise McIntyre**